# Writing Our Way Home

ESSENTIAL ANTHOLOGIES SERIES 5

 Canada Council   Conseil des Arts
for the Arts   du Canada

Guernica Editions Inc. acknowledges the support of
the Canada Council for the Arts and the Ontario Arts Council.
The Ontario Arts Council is an agency of the Government of Ontario. We
acknowledge the financial support of the Government of Canada through
the Canada Book Fund (CBF) for our publishing activities.

# Writing Our Way Home

Edited by
LICIA CANTON
and CAROLINE MORGAN DI GIOVANNI

With an introduction by Elena Lamberti

**GUERNICA**
TORONTO – BUFFALO – LANCASTER (U.K.) 2013

Copyright © 2013, the Editors, Authors, Translators,
Association of Italian Canadian Writers, and Guernica Editions Inc.
All rights reserved. The use of any part of this publication,
reproduced, transmitted in any form or by any means, electronic,
mechanical, photocopying, recording or otherwise stored in a
retrieval system, without the prior consent of the publisher is an
infringement of the copyright law.

Licia Canton & Caroline Morgan Di Giovanni, editors
Michael Mirolla, general editor
**Guernica Editions Inc.**
P.O. Box 117, Station P, Toronto (ON), Canada M5S 2S6
2250 Military Road, Tonawanda, N.Y. 14150-6000 U.S.A.

Book design by Jamie Kerry of Belle Étoile Studios
www.belleetoilestudios.com

Distributors:
University of Toronto Press Distribution,
5201 Dufferin Street, Toronto (ON), Canada M3H 5T8
Gazelle Book Services, White Cross Mills, High Town, Lancaster LA1 4XS U.K.

First edition.
Printed in Canada.

Legal Deposit – First Quarter

Library of Congress Catalog Card Number: 2013933654

**Library and Archives Canada Cataloguing in Publication**
Writing our way home / Licia Canton,
Caroline Morgan di Giovanni, editors.
(Essential anthologies series ; 5)
Also issued in electronic format.
Text mostly in English with some Italian.
ISBN 978-1-55071-802-7
1. Canadian literature (English)--Italian Canadian authors.
2. American literature--Italian American authors. 3. Italian literature.
I. Canton, Licia, 1963- II. DiGiovanni, Caroline Morgan, 1947-
III. Series: Essential anthologies series (Toronto, Ont.) ; 5

PS8235.I8W755 2013        C810.8'0851071        C2013-901375-X

*In memory of*

Anna Carlevaris (1954-2012)
Giovanni Costa (1940-2011)
John G. Madott (1918-2011)

al di là di quel vasto orizzonte
c'è un lungo acciottolato di memorie
*from the poem "Ricordi" by Giovanni Costa*

# Contents

ACKNOWLEDGEMENTS     10

INTRODUCTION     11
*Elena Lamberti*

## Part I. Understanding Identity: Theoretical Frameworks

Translating Home
*Oriana Palusci*     *21*

Migration to Exile: The Paradox of Exodus
*Ernesto Livorni*     *36*

Ways of Writing Home
*Jim Zucchero*     *43*

## Part II. Creative Visitations: Voicing Old and New Homes

Entering Sicily
*Darlene Madott*     *57*

Pastafasù
*Nino Famà*     *64*

Two Poems
*Venera Fazio*     *69*

The Funeral
*Osvaldo Zappa*     *71*

Building My Bridge Home
*Maria Lisella*     *76*

Two Poems
*Caroline Morgan Di Giovanni*     *81*

My Husband Lives in My Garage
  *Linda Morra* ................................................. 84

Growth
  *Mike Dell'Aquila* ............................................. 90

Homecoming
  *Domenic Cusmano* ............................................. 97

Dominique
  *John Calabro* ................................................ 103

Del cacciucco le code
  *Alberto Mario DeLogu* ........................................ 109

Il suono delle campane
  *Pietro Corsi* ................................................ 111

La giacca
  *Delia De Santis* ............................................. 118

America
  *Gil Fagiani* ................................................. 121

Concrete Porch, Iron Railings
  *Frank Giorno* ................................................ 123

Poems from *Random Thoughts*
  *Marisa De Franceschi* ........................................ 124

In the Stacks
  *Licia Canton* ................................................ 129

Billy
  *Michael Mirolla* ............................................. 136

## Part III. Past, Present and the Hybrid Self: Critical and Creative Considerations

Transcultural Creative Non-Fiction: Caterina Edwards' *Finding Rosa* and Janice Kulyk Keefer's *Honey and Ashes*. Finding the Way Home Through Narrative
  *Maria Tognan* ................................................ 145

Reverse Translation
  *Darlene Madott & Gianna Patriarca* ........................... 155

Nino Ricci's Mythopoiesis: Where Has <u>He</u> Gone?
  *Maria Giuseppina Cesari*   *167*

*Sweet Lemons 2*: Discovery and Memory
  *Delia De Santis & Venera Fazio*   *173*

Tra Scozia e Italia: identità, differenza e poetica interculturale in William Sharp
  *Annalisa Bonomo*   *179*

La Traversata – Italian Immigrant Accounts of Ocean Crossings
  *Michele Campanini*   *185*

CONTRIBUTORS   190

# Acknowledgements

*Writing Our Way Home* grew out of the academic and literary presentations delivered during the thirteenth biennial conference of the Association of Italian Canadian Writers (AICW), held in Atri on June 10 to 13, 2010, at Hotel Du Parc, Atri (Teramo), Italy. The conference benefitted from support provided by Centro Scuola e Cultura Italiana, Toronto; the Canadian Embassy in Rome; the Consiglio Regionale dell'Abruzzo; the city of Atri; and Hotel Du Parc. Heartfelt thanks to Alberto Di Giovanni for hosting the conference and to the conference participants for their contributions and co-operation.

For their assistance and excellent advice, we are grateful to the AICW Conference Committee members: Licia Canton, Alberto Di Giovanni, Venera Fazio, Connie Guzzo McParland, Caroline Morgan Di Giovanni, Pasquale Verdicchio and Domenic Cusmano, for his steadfast support. A special word of appreciation goes to Peter Egyed, from the Canadian Embassy in Rome. Thanks also to Giulia De Gasperi, John Partington and Erica Morassutti.

We acknowledge the support of the Association of Italian Canadian Writers, and extend our warm appreciation to Michael Mirolla and Guernica Editions for making this book possible. The Editors are grateful to the Association of Italian Canadian Writers for entrusting them with this project.

# Introduction

### *Elena Lamberti*

I REMEMBER WELL MY JOURNEY FROM Bologna, the city where I live and work, to Atri, in Abruzzo. That's where, in June 2010, the thirteenth biennial conference of the Association of Italian Canadian Writers was held. I travelled on a slow train along the Adriatic Coast. The train stops in Pineto and, from there, someone can pick you up by car or you have to wait for the right bus. It was a typical hot, Italian summer day. On that train, I couldn't help but think that even in 2010 Italy was still a country travelling at different speeds, metaphorically and literally. Travelling North to South and vice versa, Italy moves much faster along its western corridor than along the eastern one. Never mind how long it takes and how slow it is to travel from coast to coast: the railway lines that connect the Tyrrhenian Sea to the Adriatic have been the same for ages. There, through time, it is the railway that stands still, while the surrounding territory moves. A typical Italian paradox.

I was thinking of the peculiar mapping of Italian railways while going to a conference whose theme was connected to the idea of travelling: "Writing Our Way Home" or, in Italian, "Il viaggio di ritorno." That title would immediately render the idea of both a real and an imaginary journey, combining different landscapes and suggesting an open idea of 'Home,' to be questioned and assessed at the symposium. I would be listening to stories of Italians who arrived in the 'Nuovo Mondo' long ago. If truth be told, I was afraid of those stories or, rather, I was afraid I would have to listen to stories told too many times: redundant stories of Italian immigrants abroad, grown into a self-referential myth blurring the intensity of the historical archetype which had originated them. Stories that felt more and more distant from my changing self and from my modern, changing world – Italy in 2010. Don't get me wrong, I have a deep respect for the stories and history of all those who, for different reasons, were forced to leave their Motherland. (When you are forced to leave, you never leave a country; you leave a *Motherland*; a *Patria* not a nation). My respect is born out of my historical sense and my cultural memory. It is rooted in my personal knowledge of many Italian immigrants abroad whose lasting trauma and pain are also well known to me. However, I must confess that, on my way to Atri, I also couldn't help but think of the many times I had felt subtle impatience and a pervasive frustration in seeing that intense trauma imploding in a series of narrative clichés. These narrative clichés have shaped the two main characters of the early immigrant's *commedia* (or perhaps '*tragedia*') *dell'arte*: the victim (the Italian immigrant) and the persecutor (the new country). A *Mother*land, the old country cannot be a stepmother, even if it can no longer hold us close as a mother does.

Having said this, I recognize the important role of Italian-Canadian literature. Through time, determination and talent, Italian-Canadian writers have established a cultural and artistic heritage which matters to both Canada and Italy.[1] I remember the work of Raffaele Cocchi, a colleague at the University of Bologna, who was one of the first to bring new and emerging Italian-Canadian voices to our attention as early as the 1980s. Although he passed away unexpectedly in 2004, his lessons remain. His contributions to the Fondazione Giovanni Agnelli "Altreitalie," and to CISEI – Centro Internazionale Studi Emigrazione Italiana – are still landmarks in the study of the culture and history of Italians abroad. He also taught us *how* to appreciate those new works – not simply to acquire sociological knowledge about Italian emigration, but more importantly to value their intrinsic aesthetic and literary merits. Raffaele Cocchi taught us to be passionate about Italian-Canadian voices while not exempting us from a critical response and appreciation. Of course the immigrants' stories and nostalgia are traditional tenets of Italian-Canadian literature, but they can no longer be narrated in the same ways. The impatience and frustration alluded to above did not originate from a lack of appreciation for traditional themes in Italian-Canadian literature, but rather from my desire to see that literature grow and bloom. I want to see it change and face new contingent challenges because *we* change through time and history is always in the making.

In other words, as an Italian reading Italian-Canadian literature in Italy (the motherland), I maintain that today's Italian-Canadian writers could contribute much more to the literary community – which includes Italians, Canadians and all those who think that literature plays a fundamental role in our global and globalised brave new world. History has changed rather quickly: Italy is now the promised land for newcomers forced to leave their own motherland. Italy is to these new immigrants what Canada was to Italian immigrants not too long ago. It does not matter that, in fact, Italy IS NOT Canada. Yes, it's an old story: history repeats itself. What if *my own* old immigrants, as well as their literary children, those Italians who have been so successful, who have *made it*, help us (old and new Italians) to find ways of better understanding each other, our stories and our histories? After all, our Italian immigrants have been able to overcome, through literature too, all those material, cultural and social obstacles that Italian-Canadian writers and artists have so well described in their novels, poems, paintings, songs and movies. The time has come to speak *in the present* and *for the present*. It is time to listen to second and third generation children who were born in Canada and who have a different understanding of *home* and *Motherland*. That does not mean to deny history. On the contrary, it means using history wisely and speaking to Italy from Canada as Italian immigrants who suffered the same experiences not too long ago, but who were successful nonetheless. Who better than the sons and daughters who have experienced the trauma of forced immigration can talk to a mother, a nation, Italy, which is now playing the role of the persecutor in the literary works written by new *X*-Italian writers? Yes! There are new writers in Italy. They were not born in Italy, but they have a sense of belonging there. In their stories, too, there are homes, mothers and stepmothers, countries and nations. History repeats itself, but sometimes – well, often – in reverse.

Travelling on slow trains gives one time to think. Italian immigrants in the world, journeys from and to the motherland, Raffaele Cocchi and his lessons, newcomers to Italy: that's what I reflected on as I travelled from Bologna to Pineto. Once in Atri, I met the old and new voices of Italian-Canadian literature. I was comforted. My worries disappeared. I thought of Raffaelle Cocchi even more. He would have been very happy in Atri and not just because of the superb location and memorable meals. He would have been happy to witness the literature he loved so much reaching a new prime and moving on. Looking back, I dare say that the gathering in Atri was a turning point in the history of the Association of Italian Canadian Writers. As a consequence, it was a turning point in the history of the reception of Italian-Canadian literature outside of Canada, and especially in Italy. Yes, we want the best for what we love most! Atri was a good moment for the AICW: it revealed a mature literary group which is still blooming – not only in numbers (members), but mostly in themes, content, ideas. Certainly, the immigrants' stories are still being told (it goes without saying!), but nostalgia now has a different flavour. Italian-Canadian writers and scholars have assaulted, so to speak, the cliché, bringing new registers and innovating the intergenerational dialogue. It is now possible to laugh about old grievances: not to diminish them, but to turn pain into energy. It's no longer survival: it's a new, full, happy and tragic life.

Thus, going to Atri was important for me. This brief introduction is my way of writing my own way home, my way of returning to Atri – a place and a moment in time which brought something new to someone like me, who engages mostly with Canadian literature, including Italian-Canadian writing. As a matter of fact, since today's literary critics are, once again, discussing the (old) idea of world literature,[2] I would argue that Italian-Canadian writers are not just Canadian writers, but *world* writers. They write from Canada with an original point of view on multiple (hybrid) identities and have something to tell the whole world itself (which, after all, is but a cultural hybrid).

Looking back, 2010 was an important year for Italian-Canadian artists and writers at large, because of the events in Atri and other literary gatherings. For instance, in 2010 an Italian-Canadian artist, Dominic Mancuso, won the Juno Award for "World Music" for his capability to "transcend cultures and borders making old world new." Once acclaimed as a "folk" or "ethnic" artist, Mancuso is now appreciated in Canada as a "world" artist; his Sicilian rooted music has bloomed into universal heritage, crossing and embedding diversities. Following a similar path, from *Juno* to *June* 2010, the Atri conference beautifully framed three main evolving aspects of the growing AICW community: a new idea of trans-generational Italian-Canadian literature which transcends the ethnic elements and reaches universal themes; a growing presence of Italian-Canadian voices within the university "establishment," that is the growing presence of thinkers who are being established as sound mainstream critics outside the original community; the blooming of a new generation of writers and scholars, in constant critical dialogue with the previous one, who are also introducing different aesthetic experiences (for instance, the choice of writing in a language which is no longer a "hybrid," nor is it a crossroad of different sounds, but which, instead, wants to return "pure." Be it English, French or Italian, new Italian-Canadian writers often choose to write in a sole language to be different, to provoke, or simply because they do not feel that the *italiese* of the previous generations is their own language anymore).

Like my original journey by train, the journey that brings us this book was a long and slow one; just like the former, the latter too gave us all time to think, talk, and move on. The contributing writers were good travelling companions as they engaged in long and lasting conversations on the contents and form of their pieces. Their collaboration helped the editors to design a home for all ideas, feelings, and questions discussed in Atri. From a physical place (Atri), to a metaphysical place (the process which led to this volume) to another physical place (this book): this collection takes us all metaphorically back *home*, to Atri. We move back to move on, knowing that Atri further proved that travelling is but our existential condition: the identity of the AICW family is at home only when moving, that is only if we constantly question the making of our shifting identities because this association is made up of women and men who march *with* and *in* the world. This volume bears witness to that.

The three sections shaping the collection face an almost impossible challenge: to give order to the "creative and engaging" disorder of a conference. A creative disorder generated by the challenging questions nourished by the various presentations, readings, casual conversations (we know too well that many original thoughts are born out of what we discuss at coffee break or at dinner). The compromise between order and disorder is provided by the book form, which, in this case, cannot be introduced as mere conference proceedings. The three sections – "Understanding Identity: Theoretical Frameworks," "Creative Visitations: Voicing Old and New Homes," "Past, Present, and the Hybrid Self: Critical Considerations" – aim to create a narrative arc to contain the thousands of rivers of words shaping the many ideas on how to write our way home discussed at and after the conference. They take us from the journey questioning one's own identity approached through old and new theoretical frameworks read through the Italian-Canadian case, to the creative journeys of writers mapping geo-cultural dimensions across space, time and languages, to considerations cross-reading history and stories, events and memories to interpret and reinterpret literary canons and genres.

In the first section, Oriana Palusci, Ernesto Livorni and Jim Zucchero develop a theoretical framework which spans from semantic and terminological investigations of key terms to define and understand our sense of being and belonging, to a more specific mapping of the morphology of the new Italian-Canadian literature, to the investigation of the role played by various mediators of memory (i.e. memoirs, novels, poems and films) in establishing universal patterns within individual or ethnic diasporas. Language, register, tone are also investigated as rhetorical devices forming a set of formidable tools that Italian-Canadian writers have been exploring and employing to "constantly negotiat[e] the relationship between their Italian cultural heritage and their Canadian cultural experience" (Zucchero). Their contributions fit the spirit of a conference and make good use of *lightness* (in the sense indicated by Calvino in his *American Lessons*) to convey complex and thorny issues. Why should it be otherwise? Theoretical discourses are much more effective if conceived first of all as "conversations," that is, as genuine attempts to share ideas and advance thoughts. Too often, academic discourses are too far from the actual need of "common readers"; the clarity of diction and earnestness of purpose adopted by these critics here cannot but become shared tenets of all scholars joining the AICW.

In the third section, Maria Tognan, Darlene Madott & Gianna Patriarca, Maria Giuseppina Cesari, Delia De Santis & Venera Fazio, Annalisa Bonomo and Michele Campanini discuss more specific case studies, therefore proving that there are many ways to write our way home. The "creative nonfiction" of Janice Kulyk Keefer and Caterina Edwards are juxtaposed to work out shared narrative patterns bringing together the quests of different ethnic groups; similarly, the work of a canonical writer like Nino Ricci is challenged through an investigation of mythical (i.e. universal) elements in turn (re)shaping the writer's own identity quest. In dialogue with Darlene Madott, Gianna Patriarca, too, reveals how her "classic" collection of poems, *Italian Women and Other Tragedies*, is in fact an "open work": those "poems," self-translated into her native language, stay now as a never-ending journey because "poems are about language in transition," just like the human beings who read and *feel* them. Similarly, De Santis and Fazio share some feedback and considerations on their Sicilian collections; their "backstage" stories are testimony to the shift of themes within the specific community of Sicilian immigrants, therefore presenting new identity needs and new forms to express them. Sicily returns also in the contribution by Annalisa Bonomo but in an unexpected way: Sicily becomes here the home in the writings of a Scottish writer, William Sharp, to prove that, through time and space, exile and home are constant leitmotivs across literary traditions and cultures. That foreign writer, so far from us today both in time and in space, sees "the Sicilian Highlands with the beauty of Scotland": how not to think, then, that home is but within us or it is not; it depends on us to constantly find or rediscover it, bridging old and new landscapes through our imagination. Literature can make all those landscapes available through time and cultures to a multitude of different audiences engaged in their new real and metaphorical journeys. Travelling back (or forth) home is therefore an existential and suspended moment which is particularly intriguing for old and new literary explorations; it does not surprise us if, as Campanini recalls, the real journey, too, remains one of the favourite memories of immigrants abroad. No matter how painful it was, the journey is the way between, both a necessity and a choice, the act which will change forever our way of being and of belonging.

In between, the second section presents a selection of creative responses to the idea of writing our way home. Different in gender, age, education, life experience, John Calabro, Pietro Corsi, Domenic Cusmano, Mike Dell'Aquila, Alberto Mario DeLogu, Delia De Santis, Nino Famà, Venera Fazio, Maria Lisella, Darlene Madott, Caroline Morgan Di Giovanni, Linda Morra, Osvaldo Zappa, Gil Fagiani, Licia Canton and Michael Mirolla create a broad network of renderings proving that the community is alive and kicking. They engage with different genres to share their own cultural and biographical journeys and to prove that form itself is part of their own creative visitations and identities: from their lives to fiction, to poetry, to memoirs, to short stories, their works are a kaleidoscope of images, feelings, ideas which cannot but enrich (and complicate) our own lives as readers.

To an Italian like me, read as a whole these contributions seem to tell a much bigger story which both contains and transcends them all; a story which, in fact, relates to the vantage point history has granted to the AICW family. AICW writers (and scholars) have lived, rendered, studied and investigated processes of im/migration through time and from an original setting: they experienced or inherited a not too distant past of im/migration living in a country, Canada, which has chosen to transform its multiethnic dimension into a multicultural reality, as we now know with complex and evolving results. Inevitably, both their history and their Canadian location charge Italian-Canadian writers with an enormous artistic and civic responsibility. Today, they are in fact called to help old and new Italians to better understand each other. They can help us to understand the importance of acknowledging, respecting and learning from all differences. To do that, these writers and scholars can rely upon a literature that they helped grow through many differences, many experiences, languages, dialects, regionalisms; a literature that has been able to bring all those differences together and to grow through them. That literature played a role in shaping a broader group identity which was not visible before because too fragmented; that literature was able to speak to all Italians in Canada and to all Canadians alike. It is now time to make that literature speak with renewed strength to old and new Italians alike. These writers can teach the old ones how to welcome as their own children those who are now forced to leave their motherland in search of a new home; to the new ones, they can teach how to no longer portray themselves as victims, but as would be protagonists of other exciting stories. To both, they can teach that nothing is to be taken for granted, that home itself is continuous negotiations among different sensibilities. Through their works, AICW writers and scholars who met and renewed their dialogue in Atri, as well as those who added their voices after, can and must help us to shape a future full of challenges; they can and must help us to make sure that it will always be possible, for each of us, to write our way home in spite of the different speeds our trains will run at. In fact, they can and must help us to discover that we often go home and leave again without even boarding a train. A typical paradox of life.

## Notes

1. The list of works bearing witness to the strength and value of Italian-Canadian productions is by now very long. For a critical update on the different collections and anthologies, up to 2002, see the Editor's Note in *The Dynamics of Cultural Exchange*, edited by L. Canton, with an introduction by C. Verduyn and L. Canton (Montreal: Cusmano, 2002). See also C. Morgan Di Giovanni (ed.), *Bravo! A Selection of Prose and Poetry by Italian Canadian Writers* (Toronto: Quattro Books, 2012) and *Italian Canadian Voices: A Literary Anthology* (Oakville: Mosaic Press, 2006); J. Pivato (ed.), *The Anthology of Italian-Canadian Writing* (Toronto: Guernica Editions, 1998); M. De Franceschi (ed.), *Pillars of Lace* (Toronto: Guernica Editions, 1998); Canton, De Santis, Fazio (eds.), *Writing Beyond History* (Montreal: Cusmano, 2006); De Santis, Fazio, Foschi Ciampolini (eds.), *Strange Peregrinations* (Toronto: Iacobucci Centre, 2007); Canton, Fazio, Zucchero (eds.), *Reflections on Culture* (Toronto: Iacobucci Centre, 2010).

2. See, for instance: Giuliana Benvenuti, Remo Ceserani, *La letteratura nell'età globale*, Bologna: Il Mulino, 2012; Theo D'Haen, *The Routledge Concise History of World Literature*, Routledge, 2011; Eric Hayot, *On Literary Worlds*, Oxford UP, 2012.

# PART I

# Understanding Identity
*Theoretical Frameworks*

# Translating Home

*Oriana Palusci*

HOW MANY WAYS DO WE have to write home? How many homes do we have? How many homes does a Canadian have? John Slama, a Toronto writer, reminds us that, "on Canada Day, hundreds of new Canadians will take the oath, become citizens and sing 'O Canada! our home and native land!'" (2004). As a second-generation immigrant, Slama tells the story of his mother, an ethnic German born in what is now Serbia, who fled home to Germany in 1944, when the Russian army advanced westwards towards the heart of Hitler's Reich. "But home [...] proved a temporary concept for a decade. Eventually, my mother went on to earn a degree in nursing at Graz, Austria, and emigrated to Windsor, Ont., in 1961."

As Canada is a crossroad of different destinies and stories, in the sixties it was also 'home' to one of the main Canadian writers of Italian origin, Nino Ricci, who re-visited his childhood in Windsor in his very personal autobiographical essays collected in *Roots and Frontiers*, printed in Italy in a bilingual version edited by Carmen Concilio. According to Slama, who adopted a child in China, and called her Annie, "Some of us were born here, some weren't. We all call Canada home." He closes his article asserting that "home is not necessarily where you're from, but where you belong." The problem is that Canada itself, although an extraordinary multicultural national entity constitutionally based on the 1988 Multicultural Act, is bound to question itself on the meanings of the hybridity of the very process constituting its identity/identities within a multilingual society even in the twenty-first century.

This is also relevant in the context of the web of relations linking the Italian origins of many of its inhabitants to the so-called Canadian background of the North American country the *paesani* migrated to from the end of the nineteenth century and especially after the Second World War. Some Canadians have decided to cut the umbilical cord with the land of their ancestors, even if the Italian surname they carry still echoes a feeble, yet recognizable link with their ancient cradle. Other Canadians cling to their land of birth and/or to their ancestors refusing to erase a past rooted elsewhere. Canadian writers of Italian origin experience in their writings a "clash of discourses," as Barbara Godard would say, signalling in different degrees their "displacement of identity and language" (1990: 154). Thus, notions of national identity are subjected to a continual negotiation with a home still existing (and developing) elsewhere.

The first question concerns the naming of these writers: ethnic, Italic, Italian writers in exile, Italian-Canadian, Canadian of Italian origin or just Canadian writers? What is clear is that cultural traditions and languages collide in their literary texts, producing a continuous effect of estrangement, of foreignness, of translation. I am aware that in the now rich panorama of Anglo-Canadian writers of Italian origin from coast to coast each writer deploys a specific kit of techniques difficult to place in one homogenous frame.

However, by the end of the twentieth century, Antonio D'Alfonso had warned against the spectre of assimilation, yet willing to domesticate the 'foreign' side of the hyphen:

> [...] [I]t is all right to be an Italian Canadian just as long as Italian eventually melts totally into the Canadian side of the hyphen. The problem is that this Canadian side is just as confused as the other side of the equation. Like any other country in America, there is no such thing as a Canadian. It is too vague a term to encompass all that the term implies. [...] Even if there were such a thing as a Canadian; that is, a Canadian hyphen Canadian, it would be no better or worse than any other hyphenated group. A Canadian Canadian in Canada is just one of the many ethnic groups in the country (2006: 239).

D'Alfonso, a plurilingual and pluricultural writer, is well aware of the intricacies of a concept which in Quebec is called "interculturalism" (obviously this is his translation) and in English Canada "multiculturalism" (*Ibid.*: 238), because, as a second-generation immigrant, whose parents had moved from a small village in Molise (Ricci's family did migrate from a similar background), he had to cope with the two hegemonic cultures and languages of his parents' new home, while exploring other North American linguistic stratifications. Therefore, in the rich linguistic mélange of his poem *Babel* he writes:

> Nativo di Montréal
> élevé comme Québécois
> forced to learn the tongue of power
> vivì en México como alternativa
> figlio del sole e della campagna
> par les franc-parleurs aimé
> finding thousands like me suffering
> me casé y divorcié en tierra fria
> nipote di Guglionesi
> parlant politique magré moi
> *steeled in the school of Old Aquinas*
> queriendo luchar con mis amigos latinos
> Dio where shall I be demain
> (trop vif) qué puedo saber yo
> Spero che la terra be mine
>
> *(D'Alfonso 1998: 195)*

Although D'Alfonso calls his poem *Babel*, the biblical reference does not necessarily convey a negative overtone, underscoring, instead, that Canada is a cultural, more than a political, formation, a metaphorical house of translation. For D'Alfonso, translation is at the core of the Canadian cultural awareness, in the sense that Homi Bhabha locates within the broader horizon of postcolonial studies: "It is the dream of translation as survival [...] an empowering condition of hybridity" (1994: 324).

In the context of the Italian-Canadian consciousness, the crucial issue is about Italian roots that cannot and should not be totally eradicated, but at the same time they are in danger of becoming imprisoned in the poetics of nostalgia or, on the other hand, of being oversimplified in the cage of naïve, harmless, old-fashioned stereotypes. "It is only when ethnic collectivities overcome the private nostalgia and the rear-view vision of culture of the first-generation immigrants that the serious incorporation of cultures can begin." (D'Alfonso 2006: 243) *Incorporation* here means, according to me, *translation* of a culture within a dominant language, not only on a broadly thematic level, but also through a series of interventions on the matrix language (the language selected in the practices of writing, that is English or French) such as code-switching, borrowing and lexical dissemination of the embedded language (Italian or one of its dialects). *Babel* is, among other things, a linguistic experiment, on the one hand, on the plurality of four conflicting languages in a plurilingual society and, on the other, paradoxically, on the need to adopt a matrix language in which to operate a cultural translation. The transfer of cultural realities in a new territory (geographical and linguistic) deploys a translation effect – to use Barbara Godard's words – which relies on an overt process of defamiliarization (1990: 157). The translation effect germinates inside the text, allowing it to highlight the visible and vivid performance of languages and cultures in the plural. The performativity of diasporic subjects is accordingly represented within the texture of the matrix language, so as to stage difference, plurality, fluidity. The estrangement effect emphasizes fragments of selves through code-switching and code-mixing as if they were otherwise untranslatable.

It is as if what Lawrence Venuti (the most widely discussed and cited translation scholar in the last years) defines as foreignization (against domestication) found a privileged outcome when Canadian hyphenated writers of Italian origin are concerned. Domestication, translation at all costs according to Venuti, entails a reduction of the foreign text to the cultural values of the target language, at the same time minimizing the foreignness; while foreignization implies "to register the linguistic and cultural difference of the foreign text, sending the reader abroad." (1995: 20) Venuti also calls this attitude a strategy of resistance. Canadian multicultural literature (I am referring to the anthology edited by Smaro Kamboureli in 1996) does make a difference in the national consciousness. The degree of foreignness is what is at stake.

The impact of Italian migrants on Canada is marked by a long chain of events based on the defence of an old national identity, denying or obscuring the sturdy regional and provincial roots of each individual. During Fascism, the Italian community in Toronto needed "an articulate and regularly-published Italian-language newspaper," as Angelo Principe points out (1999: 85). Consequently, on 20 September 1929, the editorial of the first issue of *Il Bollettino italo-canadese* stated that the new newspaper:

> [...] is for the Italians or, better, for the emigrants. We seize every opportunity to assert our "Italianness" in this foreign land; but we intend to cooperate with local authorities in order that our countrymen know the laws governing this country. And that people of other nationalities will firmly understand that Italians have been, are and

will always be bearers of civilization, wherever they settle. (Principe 1999: 85-86)

As a matter of fact, from the balcony of Palazzo Venezia, Mussolini would conjure up once again, while announcing the declaration of war to France and Great Britain (and thus also Canada), a mythical "Italia ... forte, fiera e compatta" (*Discorso di Mussolini*, 10 June, 1940).

In 1957 the popular Italian song "Casetta in Canadà," interpreted by the popular melodic singer Gino Latilla, created the image of an overtly simplified North American country, even more distant and certainly less dangerous than the Unites States, where the fertility of the land and the abundance of woods enhanced the search for a better life, and promised a thriving domestic environment: "Aveva una casetta piccolina in Canadà," with its endless refrain on the reconstruction of the burnt down house. Such a perspective, partly questioned by the fact that most migrants (but not all of them) did settle in densely populated urban areas and especially in Toronto, Montreal and Vancouver, was certainly encouraged by the poignant experience of the "war brides," themselves Canadian icons, young evergreen – and Italian – girls who had met Canadian soldiers fighting in Italy with the Allied forces and travelled to Canada after the war in order to meet their boyfriends and would-be husbands.

After the Second World War, during the great immigration flows of the 1950s, when the nationalistic vision dwindled and Fascism was substituted by the Italian Republic, the theme of nostalgia of homecoming gained terrain and vigour. Nostalgia was/would be also employed to describe a land which was not even Italian anymore, as in the case of the poem by Gianni Grohovaz, *Quando me meto a scriver queste robe* in which the dialectical poet cries the loss of Fiume, an ancient Italian city lost to the new boundaries of Yugoslavia.

The search for home and the place to which one feels he/she always belongs is not an easy matter. The themes of diaspora and estrangement are the foundations of the contemporary world and resound in many of the words of its outstanding intellectuals. Hence, in an interview with Maurizio Ferraris, in speaking about his experiences as a boy during the Second World War, the influential philosopher Jacques Derrida stated: "I am a Jew from Algeria, from a certain type of community, in which belonging to Judaism was problematic, belonging to Algeria was problematic, belonging to France was problematic, etc. So all this predisposed me to non-belonging [...]" (Derrida 2001).

For second-generation immigrants like D'Alfonso, the prospective did change also because the images of a stereotypical Italian country became stronger and stronger. The post-Second World War migration from Italy to Canada was made of largely fabled expectations, a rather unsatisfactory comparison between the American and the Canadian ways of life and the confusing mixture of diversified Italian dialects and traditions. It is also true that Canada was generally considered a second choice for many Italian migrants who where unable to settle in the United States. Such an experience is related by Nino Ricci in "Going to the Moon," published in 1990: the writer's great uncle Bert had "smuggled into Canada after he'd been turned away at New York" (2006: 40), lived in Windsor, and never set foot in 'real' America. In fact, the luckiest and most respected members of Ricci's family prospered beyond the border, in Ohio, USA, although, during the Vietnam War, Benny, one of his cousins, lost his life in combat, so that, for his relatives, the blessing of the American citizenship collapsed under the heavy burden of mourning and sorrow.

Ricci's life, as reshaped by the Canadian author in his autobiographical essays collected in *Roots and Frontiers*, witnesses the growth of a multi-layered identity, partly Italian, partly Canadian. Nino Ricci was born in Canada in 1959, six years after his parents migrated from a remote village in Molise to Leamington, Ontario. Moving later to Windsor, within easy eyeshot of the USA border, the young boy would wistfully observe the dense smoke rising from the car factories in Detroit. The writer encapsulates the desire of an unreachable American dream in the strong Catholic (even Dantesque) image of Windsor as a temporary Purgatory:

> Windsor seemed a kind of purgatory to me, a temporary stop between whatever hell my parents had left behind in Italy and the vague promise of the skyline that opened up beyond the Detroit River. (Ricci 2003: 40)

Ricci narrates how he was raised in an Italian milieu, sent to a Catholic school, where American values were firmly on the foreground (as in the event of a failed expedition to the moon, followed eagerly by all the schoolmates under the guidance of motherly Miss Johnson), consequently making the schoolboy, with Italian parents, an outsider, "moving uncertainly through a world that refused to admit us [he and his brother], that we had to hide ourselves within like animals changing the colour of their fur to fit into a landscape" (2003: 44). His birth in Canada is perceived by the author as a mere accident, something which makes him an awkward, cumbersome, obtrusive *lusus naturae*, despised also by his older, more integrated brother. Thus, in his autobiographical pieces, Ricci explores the growing consciousness of a youth carefully mapping cartography of feelings, recruiting the language of affect in a land which increasingly reveals dystopian overtones. The Italian subject examines the self in terms of dissonance, of conflict, of social anxiety.

All Ricci's relatives are Italian, and the domestic arrangements are influenced by the consciousness of a cherished Italian way of life. Ricci's house in Windsor is itself a sort of replica of a pristine Italian dwelling he had never personally inhabited. The reader is invited to enter the *sala da pranzo*, which his mother – writes Nino – "guarded as an avenging angel":

> A tall china cabinet stood in one corner, housing small arrangements of silverware and copper pots that emerged from behind their glass doors only for their monthly cleaning; and on the cabinet's top, underneath a clear glass dome, sat a golden pendulum clock which my mother wound every Sunday after church with a special key, bringing an old chair in from the kitchen to reach it and setting aside its dome with a **tenderness** that seemed oddly out of keeping with the ruddiness of her hands, with the hard set of her shoulders and chin. (Ricci 2003: 42)

The writer recalls how his parents tried to reproduce an archetypal Italian abode, making it better, larger, more comfortable, but still a self-sustained space, a sort of island in the middle of a foreign country, a dis-located home, de-centred and full of familiar echoes. As we see in the above quotation, the writer employs one of the main strategies in the cultural translation of home, that is the recurrence to the language of affect – *tenderness* – here applied to his mother.

On the other hand, one of his relatives, Uncle Luigi, according to Ricci's memoirs in "Passage to Canada," gives up the idea of a proper place where to live, in order to save money and arrange his journey back to Italy as soon as possible. At the small farming town of Leamington on the north shore of Lake Erie, Uncle Luigi's Lilliputian cabin suggests the artificial and temporary nature of the Canadian experience, a mere gap to be superseded by the craved restoration of the 'real' Italian order:

> We used to visit him sometimes Sunday mornings after mass and he always seemed so settled and self-sufficient and in his element in that elfin habitation, with his army-sized cot and his stoop-shouldered

> Kelvinator fridge and the little shot glasses he'd bring out for a glass of Tia Maria or **anisette**. It was a kind of shock to me as I grew older to learn that he had this completely other life across the sea that he would be returning to, and that everything here, his blackened **espresso** pot, his tiny sloped-ceilinged rooms, was merely provisional, a way station. I had not quite understood then this dual-sidedness of imagination, how there was always an absent reference point that the present stood against, and that could make the present's nuts-and-bolts everydayness and permanence suddenly appear the merest shadow. (Ricci 2003: 76, *emphasis mine*)

Culture bound words in Italian – *anisette, espresso* – function as objects of desire slightly opening, or not totally closing, the door home. They are loanwords that semantically charge the text with cultural references targeted to a self-conscious Italian readership in Canada.

When, as a young man, Ricci visits the country of his ancestors, he meets a very different kind of civilization and a new village community, and must adapt his perception to the sense of difference that the ancient, narrow buildings project on him. It is very difficult for him to define where his own *home* is: both the lost world of childhood in Canada, recollected and translated by a true full-blooded Italian young man born in exile, and the re-discovered world of his rural Italian ancestors, seem to deny the fullness of a total identification. Home is a very elusive concept, indeed, because the journey towards home has no clear bearing, and the writer is like Alice in Wonderland, vainly questioning the Cheshire Cat about the right direction.

In the short story "The Fountain," Ricci tells the story of a well-integrated Italian community living in the imaginary small town of Mersea. When the community is required to participate in the celebrations of the Centennial of the city, one of its mentors, the young Tony Rossi, plans a beautiful fountain, modelled on the ancient monuments he has dug out in art books found in the city library. The local Roma Club detects the assets and liabilities of the project, splitting into two different factions, led by Tony Rossi and by his opponent Dino Mancini. Although it is clear that Tony had not considered a certain number of topical problems (How would the other citizens react to the naked women sculptured in the original models? What would happen to the streaming water during the harsh Canadian winter?). Eventually the fountain is built. On viewing it for the first time, Tony realizes it is a crude pastiche of several incongruous materials and styles. Moreover, he has to overcome several obstacles to fill the fountain with a stream of water. Finally, an unknown hand throws a box of laundry soap in the water: "[A]nd a night of churning had built up this landscape of foam" (Ricci 1998: 243). There is no way to repeat the glories of the past and the Mersea Italian community does not achieve any glorious unity of intent and perspectives: Dino's faction, in fact, exploits the Roma Club to achieve a broader social recognition and is not really interested in the celebration of the Italian past. Yet, the bronze goddess on the top of the fountain is still clearly visible over the chaotic mess of bubbles. It reminds Tony of "Venus [...], the goddess of love, rising up from the foam of the sea" (*Ibid*. 244). Inadvertently, Tony has created a new, ironical version of an old myth, a very ephemeral and casual body of art renewing and translating an obsolete tradition into a sort of postmodern – or maybe a post-national – pastiche.

In this sort of cultural battlefield, new ideas clash with the old ones and stereotypes of the Italian past survive, while next-generation migrants try to break the mould, to adhere to a new identity, to new individual needs and desires. The debate on the translation of one's name from Italian into English is a common strategy in many texts, juxtaposing the new self and the new culture, with the old one often located in the everyday life routine. For instance, in C.D. Minni's emblematic short story "Details from the Canadian Mosaic" (1980), Mario, the young protagonist, is displaced from his native village to follow his family to the Canadian Pacific coast. Eager to be accepted, he becomes a hybrid subject once he adapts to the target language by translating his own name, for the new environment, in a sort of awkward familiarization:

> He did not know at what point he had become Mike. One day looking for a suitable translation of his name and finding none, he decided that Mike was closest. By the end of summer, he was Mario at home and Mike in the streets. (Minni 1980: 56)

Naming in Italian often highlights the characters' hybridity as well as their foreignness. Inside the Canadian English text Italian names create an estrangement effect, while functioning as memory tokens which resist forgetfulness, a few precious gems sparkling in an ocean of English words. The use of Italian names for the characters, with the consequent link to Italian place-names and culture-bound words, responds to a specific technique of defamiliarization, through the strategic use of specific names embodying a symbolic meaning recognizable only for the readers of Italian origin. They are names from home transplanted elsewhere. Among the many examples, the first that comes to mind is *Rita Latte*, the protagonist of Mary di Michele's novel *Under My Skin*, published in 1994, or *Immacolata*, the character in Patriarca's eponymous poem from *My Etruscan Face* (2007):

> Immacolata came into my
> class at age nine
> she was all her name implied
> immaculate
>     beautiful
>         smart
>
> because we shared a mother country
> i made an assumption
> unwise
>
> "Immacolata,
> that is a beautiful name
> but would you rather I called you
> by a shorter name, something easier
> like Maggie?"
>
> her sinuous black eyes gazed
> at me without reservation
>
> "my name is Immacolata, call me
> Immacolata"
>
> but i should have known that (2007: 58).

In this case, a very young Italian girl defies assimilation (suggested by another Italian individual, the poet herself in her role as school teacher) and proudly declares that the 'foreign' name (*Immacolata*), difficult to pronounce, defines a precise ethnic identity not to be reduced to the friendly and colloquial English nickname Maggie. All the cultural implications of Immacolata – from one of the names of the Virgin to the idea of female purity – are definitely untranslatable.

The very title of a literary work can be in Italian, as in the case of *Mambo Italiano* (2001), a play by Steve Galluccio – a Montrealer of Italian origin, writing in English – later adapted into film. The main character, Angelo, a writer himself, discusses with his friend and male lover Nino about the different stereotypes stifling the richness of the Italian tradition. Both Angelo and Nino quarrel about the love/hate relationship they have with their very conservative parents:

> Nino: Stop shitting on Italians.
> Angelo: I don't shit on Italians.
> Nino: You're the classic self-hating Italian.
> Angelo: I'm not!
> Nino: Please, the way you portray Italians in your plays...it's disgraceful.
> Angelo: The truth hurts.
> Nino: Italians have greatly contributed to civilization. WE have given the world Michelangelo, Fellini, the pizza –
> Angelo: – Mussolini, the Mafia, garlic breath (2001: 28-29).

Being a homosexual, Angelo will inevitably upset his old-fashioned and sturdy Italian parents with his *outing*, while his lover falls back to a safer system of life and marries a former schoolmate, a rich and determined young woman of Italian origin. Yet, once again, although traditional values seem to be utterly useless and even false, the real problem is that also in the past, even in the family past belonging to an archaic society, one can find the traces of subversive feelings and behaviours. From the very background of his Italian family, Angelo conjures up the mythical figure of a strange Venus, his aunt Yolanda, who had committed suicide thirty years before. She used to mambo (an exotic dance reminding the spectators of Silvana Mangano's seductive performance in the 1954 film *Mambo*, directed by Robert Rossen), instead of performing the ancient folk dance Tarantella:

> But then I thought of my Aunt Yolanda, on my way [to his first gay pride], my sweet Aunt Yolanda, on that day, and remembered that, when everyone was still dancing the Tarantella, she died, trying to teach them how to Mambo. (*Ibid.*: 126)

As Galluccio points out in his tragicomic play, highly based on humour, stereotypes about food, the perfect family, the protective role of mothers are generated inside the Italian community in Montreal, before being imposed by the Canadian experience at large. They articulate the deeply-felt answer to the drama of origins, of the departure, of the journey across the ocean, of the dramatic settlement in a foreign country. The gay son, Angelo – more of a Caravaggesque angel, than a guardian angel – bitterly rebukes his parents, because the "only worthwhile thing you ever did was leave that spit of a village of yours in Italy to come here" (*Ibid.*: 86). Then he bitterly adds:

> But you never really left. 'Cause when you came here, you brought that little spit of a village along and dropped it on this country, in

your houses like a big pile of bricks. And we were forced to live there too. In 1950s Italy. With all the gossip, and the jealousy, and the lies. (*Ibid.*)

Still, something is slowly moving and changing. As Angelo's mother Maria comments, near the end of the play: "I guess we're not all tragedy, guilt and fear, after all" (*Ibid.*: 121). Thus, while Yolanda, who committed suicide as an act of liberation from the constraints of a dull marriage, and whose grave Maria and her husband visit before the end of the play, now rests in peace, the unhappy Angelo will march in the Gay Pride Parade, at least temporarily reconciled with "all the voices, all the memoirs, all the victories, all the defeats" (*Ibid.*: 125) of his troublesome life on Jean-Talon, Little Italy, Montreal, Canada.

In any case, we would like to consider Yolanda as a symbolic figure leading us towards the final stage of this paper, the one taking into consideration the strong impact of gender on the Italian-Canadian culture and especially on the poetry of women such as Mary di Michele and Gianna Patriarca, that is a poetry writing home in Canadian English, but also enriching the language with the rhythms and interpolations of an Italian linguistic background. A poetry, I might say, that is Canadian without the need to be pushed back to the old worn-out Italian-Canadian ethnic marker and, at the same time, could be defined as fully Italian, or "Italic," in D'Alfonso's words (2005: 263).

Such a poetical language overcomes and transforms both entrenched stereotypes and the most personal memories, embodying what we called the poetics of nostalgia and the new meanings of life rising from an everyday experience that is no longer foreign, estranged, belonging to the deepest levels of consciousness. Both Mary di Michele and Gianna Patriarca were born in Italy, both struggle with their background and with the complexities and challenges of their personal stories, with their expectations and disappointments, haunted by the sense of the past.

In Mary di Michele's "Life is Theatre: Or, O to Be Italian in Toronto Drinking Cappuccino on Bloor Street at Bersani and Carlevale's," poetry and experience blend together and the everlasting Italian background is morphed into an ironical discourse on the failure of love filtered through a feminine perspective. In this poem, based on the male/female dichotomy and on ethnic cultural differences, translation is conjured up as a cultural aid for the Italian migrant. The clash of occasional words in Italian typographically intruding in italics in the Canadian English text entails the depth of underground roots still retrieving old habits and culinary traditions. Food imagery exposes the dynamic tension between cultures the newcomer has to reluctantly face. In the first stanzas the *you* refers to the necessity of a word to word translation:

> You needed an illustrated dictionary
> to translate your meals, looking to the glossary
>
> of vegetables, *melanzane* became eggplant,
> African with the dark sensuality of liver.
> But for them even eggplants were exotic
> or alien, their purple skins from outer space.
> Through the glass oven door
> you would watch it bubbling in pyrex,
> layered with tomato sauce and cheese,
> *melanzane alla parmigiana* (1986: 45)

In the poetic closure, *you* shifts to *he*, to a Canadian who appropriates the Other by shouting: "*For you Italians!* [...] *life is theatre!*"

New literary styles and paradigms emerge, and they seem to bury a past which relentlessly keeps on re-surfacing. A new sense of irony and displacement redefines the concept of *home* located neither in the Italian land of the ancestors nor in the streets of Toronto's Little Italy, where Gianna Patriarca has been living for fifty years. Patriarca, a poet who has tried to write verses not only in Canadian English, but also in Italian and in her native Ciociaro, has self-translated a collection of poems into Italian (*Donne italiane e altre tragedie*). In *Italian Women and other Tragedies,* Patriarca draws a rich gallery of female characters far from their homeland. The common denominator for all diasporic peoples is not only, as Naipaul would say, the enigma of arrival, but the trauma of departure, the leaving of one's home behind, the travel by water. In "Returning" Patriarca centre-stages the traumatic detachment of the poetic voice from the concept of motherland, as motherland cannot be connected anymore to an idea of nation/nationality:

> We don't discuss the distance anymore
> Returning is now
> The other dream
> Not American at all
> Not Canadian or Italian
> It has lost its nationality. (1996: 21)

This is what is left to the migrant diasporic subjects, the Italians turning into Canadians: the sometimes nostalgic search for an unreachable, yet still vibrating living past, and the awareness that they belong to a new world in which they fit, but will never totally fit properly, marginalized figures of resistance questioning their identity through narratives and structures made of words, reinventing the language of affect. The issues of power, of gender, of ethnicity come to the fore together, reshaped through a language, Canadian English, giving voice to an identity, which is culturally marked, loaded with the memory of shreds of a permanent unforgettable ancestral past.

Could we suggest that for both Mary di Michele and Gianna Patriarca, as well as for other female and male authors, who are first-generation or second-generation migrants with roots in Italy, translating home is the re-discovery of the creative power of writing?

Writing the way home does not mean simply to include ethnographic and linguistic items or themes into the Canadian culture (which is by its own nature, already highly layered), but to *traghettare* (one of the meanings of *tradurre*) a series of experiences, narratives and linguistic devices enriching and re-defining a multicultural and multiethnic 'national' tradition. Hence, the house of the ancestors does not completely disappear, once it finds a new home in Canadian literature.

## Works Cited

Bhabha, Homi. *The Location of Culture*, New York, Routledge, 1994.

D'Alfonso, Antonio. "Babel" in Joseph Pivato, ed., *The Anthology of Italian-Canadian Writing*, Toronto, Guernica, 1998, p. 195.

_____. *Gambling with Failure*, Toronto, Exile Editions, 2006.

Derrida, Jacques. "I Have a Taste for the Secret," Interview with Maurizio Ferraris, in Jacques Derrida, Maurizio Ferraris, *A Taste for the Secret,* trans. Giacomo Donis, ed. by Donis and David Webb, Cambridge, Polity Press, 2001.

Di Michele, Mary. "Life is Theatre" in *Immune to Gravity*, Toronto, McClelland and Stewart, 1986, pp. 45-47.

Galluccio, Steve. *Mambo Italiano*, Vancouver, Talonbooks, 2001.

Godard, Barbara. "The Discourse of the Other: Canadian Literature and the Question of Ethnicity," *The Massachusetts Review*, XXI, 1990: 1-2, pp. 153-184.

Kamboureli, Smaro. *Making a Difference: Canadian Multicultural Literature*, Toronto, Oxford University Press, 1996.

Minni, C.D. "Details from the Canadian Mosaic" in *Other Selves*, Toronto, Guernica, 1985, pp. 49-57.

Patriarca, Gianna. "Returning" in *Italian Women and Other Tragedies*, Toronto, Guernica, 1996, pp. 21-22.

Patriarca, Gianna. "Immacolata" in *My Etruscan Face*, Thornhill (Ont.), Quattro Books, p. 58.

Principe, Angelo. *The Darkest Side of the Fascist Years. The Italian-Canadian Press: 1920-1942*, Toronto, Guernica, 1999.

Ricci, Nino. "The Fountain" in Joseph Pivato, ed., *The Anthology of Italian-Canadian Writing*, Toronto, Guernica, 1998, pp. 215-244.

Ricci, Nino. "Going to the Moon" and "Passage to Canada" in *Roots and Frontiers: Radici e frontiere*, edited by Carmen Concilio, Torino, Tirrenia Stampatori, 2003, pp. 40-55 and pp. 74-91.

Slama, John. "My All-Canadian Family," *MacLean's*, July 1, 2004, p. 94.

Venuti, Lawrence. *The Translator's Invisibility: A History of Translation*, London, Routledge, 1995.

# Migration to Exile: The Paradox of Exodus

*Ernesto Livorni*

As we gather here, in this attractive and well-lit room, on this cold December evening, to discuss the plight of the writer in exile, let us pause for a minute and think of some of those who, quite naturally, didn't make it to this room. Let us imagine, for instance, Turkish *Gastarbeiters* prowling the streets of West Germany, uncomprehending or envious of the surrounding reality. Or let us imagine Vietnamese boat people bobbing on high seas or already settled somewhere in the Australian outback. Let us imagine Mexican wetbacks crawling the ravines of Southern California, past the border patrols into the territory of the United States. Or let us imagine shiploads of Pakistanis disembarking somewhere in Kuwait or Saudi Arabia, hungry for menial jobs the oil-rich locals won't do. Let us imagine multitudes of Ethiopians trekking some desert on foot into Somalia (or is it the other way around?), escaping famine. Well, we may stop here, because that minute of imagining has already passed, although a lot could be added to this list. Nobody has ever counted these people and nobody, including the UN relief organizations, ever will: coming in millions, they elude computation and constitute what is called – for want of a better term or a higher degree of compassion – migration.

AT THE BEGINNING OF HIS acceptance speech for the Nobel Prize for Literature aptly titled "The Condition We Call Exile," Joseph Brodsky lists a long line of people who face the dangers of migration, even illegal means of migration, as they seek better conditions for their lives.[1] The situation that Brodsky describes evidently includes and overcomes the much more specific one of the relation between Italy and America: the phenomenon of migration from Italy to the American continent is part of that worldwide phenomenon to which Brodsky refers and of which the Italian population is only a small portion. However, the origin of things, even in the mere form of birth, accompanies and persecutes everyone; with it and implicit in it, the consciousness of the end also travels, even in the mere form of death. But between an origin lost in the darkness of time and an end yet to come there dwells the journey and the sense of its own movement. For those born in a place and migrated to another that journey is more than tangible, it is a living moment within them: for those born in Italy and migrated to America, that journey is like a deep wake of a ship that does not close itself, does not heal.

Emigration is a phenomenon that presupposes another one that is opposite and complementary to that: immigration. But in a reciprocal deletion of the two prefixes, that which remains constant and unaltered is not so much the privileged perspective of the movement from one place to another, but rather the very idea of movement: migration. Migration (from Latin *migratio*) indicates a change of location, whether definitive or temporary, that groups of human beings and animals experience from one place to another and that is determined by several reasons, but inevitably by a necessity of life. In this phenomenon one must contemplate the individual experience as well, even when it implies the departure from one's own land.

"Settembre: andiamo, è tempo di migrare" writes D'Annunzio, but that pastoral community created in the communion of "noi" gets loose already in the following line ("ora i miei pastori lascian gli stazzi"), finding its definitive sanction in the final line: "Ah, perché non son io coi miei pastori?" The answer, left in the blank page, tells us that the poet does not migrate with his shepherds because he has already gone through that experience and now he is, alone, on the road to exile.[2]

Exile (from Latin *ex(s)ilium*), instead, plunges us into the mystery already with its own etymology: Cassiodorus explains that "*ex solo enim ire est, quasi exsolium.*" This uncertain etymology will significantly resurface at the end of this discourse; for the time being, let us list the most common meanings that the term assumes in our language. Exile is a form of punishment aiming at limiting the freedom of individuals by sending them away from their homeland. This departure, on the other hand, may be a voluntary one, whether one needs to escape from punishment or violence or other reasons. Finally, exile is the very act and period of living away from the place where one would like to be. The last meaning leads to a metaphysical understanding of exile: earthly existence opposed to the eternal life in the heavenly homeland.

"In exitu Israel de Aegypto / cantavan tutti insieme ad una voce / con quanto di quell salmo è poscia scripto" writes Dante in *Purgatorio* II, 46-48, as he describes the souls brought by boat from the river Tiber to the island of Purgatory. Psalm CXIII alludes to the exodus of the people of Israel from Egypt. The exit from Egypt marks for the people of Israel the beginning of Exodus, the journey toward the Promised Land: the chant of the people of Israel is that very last chant that Aristotle, calling it indeed exodus, inserts among the parts of the tragedy, that final part that follows the so-called *stasimon*. To be sure, it is just the idea of tragedy that today overwhelms us when we observe the exodus of entire populations in our contemporary societies, including of course the exodus of Italians to America. From the exodus of Israel, that is, from the exodus of that which in the Old Testament is the people *par excellence*, we have shifted to a quite different metaphor, we have moved to the mass exodus, a definition that strives to highlight, even unjustly, the amorphous status of that which is still a human tragedy, degrading its value in that connotation of mass. Exodus is by now a metaphor used to connote migration, but we must point out the atrocious deceit that this metaphor masks: exodus presupposes not only the exit from a hostile place, from the captivity in which the people of Israel was relegated, an exit then that sets itself as point of departure for a journey, but it also presupposes a point of arrival to a privileged place: the Promised Land.

From the time in which Moses' people, after crossing the parted waters of the Red Sea, travelled through the desert, getting lost and finding itself again, until it arrived at the Land of Canaan, the Promised Land, the land of the ancestors, this place has reached a first connotation that exalts its status of paradox. The Promised Land has become the privileged metaphor in order to define utopia, in other words, that vision that, in its projection toward the future, highlights in its own etymology the absence of any place. Even Thomas More, who coined the term, pairs it with another term, eutopia, which marks the shift from the absence of place to the goodness of place.

The migrants who left from the Mediterranean and Atlantic seaports considered America a Promised Land, and therefore a good place, eutopia. The migrants of the South Seas, looking at the seacoasts of Brazil or Argentina, must have lived more or less with awareness of the myth of El Dorado, stripping it away from the sleep of past oblivion, dressing it with different deeds than those of the "conquistadores," turning history upside down in one of those reversals that make it nevertheless so fascinating. Instead, the migrants of America (especially United States and Canada) went through the desert of the Atlantic Ocean with the mirage of the Promised Land, "terra buona e vasta, terra che stilla latte e miele" (Exodus 3, 8). Perhaps the final scene in the film *Nuovomondo* (*Golden Door*, 2006) by Emanuele Crialese, in which the main characters of the film swim in milk after their arrival at Ellis Island, alludes to this biblical metaphor.

At first it would seem that the journey of the migrant, with departure travel and arrival in that which may be considered the Promised Land, proceeds hand in hand with the Jewish people in the book of Exodus, so much so that this situation justifies the aforementioned metaphor of the mass exodus often adopted to indicate the massive phenomenon of migration. But there is an important distinction to bring to the surface of this discourse about the path of the migrant: the land from which the migrant leaves is indeed the land of the fathers; it is not the place of captivity, but the privileged place from which one moves away rather than returning to it, from which one moves to exile rather than returning to it reconciled. This is the atrocious paradox of the exodus of migration: it marks the deepest laceration, that which separates a (migrant) body from another body (the place that made us, that has placed us in a community with other beings). This paradox marks the absolute displacement, separating us from the place from which we sprang out and throwing us high, with the effect of a terrible vertigo in its desperate reality and truth.

In other words, at the end of the journey, having divided the waters of the Ocean, having arrived finally on its banks, the migrant understands that (like an image reflected in a convex mirror, which reflects and yet deforms, in an illusory perspective, so that reality gains unreal dimensions) a reversal has been triggered: America is the reversal of the Promised Land. At this point, it is necessary to open a parenthesis on the very term 'America.' As it defines a continent of vast proportions, of which it is common to underline the double aspect in its division between North and South (without forgetting that delicate yet vital strip of land that goes under the name of Central America), the term 'America' would seem to belong to a neutral level of the language, merely geographical, topographical. But it is this very topography, this location of America that has contributed to the fascination with this continent: since Christopher Columbus the New World was also the other world, the world of hope, soon that of progress.

Therefore, America was the place of the future, the place yet to come, in other words the place of utopia and eutopia.

Actually, the term 'America' would connote in this respect no place on earth and yet it would remain a mere geographical notion; but we know all too well the mystification of the term. Inserted in a phrase to indicate a state, a specific body politic, the United States of America (a cumbersome presence especially for countries on its borders such as Canada and Mexico), one notices how often, almost always, the first part of the phrase is deleted, especially in political speeches or TV commercials. In this way, the term 'America' gains a specific connotation, once again founded on mystification. In fact, it is the world of history that absorbs and gives an ideological value to the otherwise geographical name, masking it in such a way as to present a political state as the state, the place in which to be, to which to belong, of which to be part, in which to compose oneself. In other words, in this apparently innocuous semantic operation, history places myth at its service and it is the migrant, who had assumed myth as guide, that remains deceived. In light of this new perspective that the migrant may assume, the statement that America is the reversal of the Promised Land acquires a more profound meaning.

The exodus has not allowed the migrant to reach the much desired Promised Land and the migrant is finally aware of his path, of that trajectory that has actually sent him away from his Land of Canaan, rather than bringing him there. Only at the moment of arrival, at the end of the journey, of this upside down exodus, can it be that migration, with all its social aspects and causes, with all its baggage of history, may be transcended by the migrant in a much wider visionary perspective. It is this new view of one's own condition as migrant that must develop strength in order to elevate itself from the algae in that new ocean of quotidian life, from those algae that, gathered along the path, wrap and tie and slow down the migrant. The migrant understands that migration has taken him to exile, to an existence in a *hic and nunc* dimension that is alien to him, in which he cannot recognize himself or herself fully. However, this condition becomes for the migrant one of privilege: he can turn back to look at the bank that has thrown him in that trajectory of migration. In fact, seen from the place of dislocation [displacement], the parabola of the exodus, with its perfect symmetry of departure, travel, and arrival, with its rising toward a climactic moment and its consequent decline, mirrors another tremendous parabola, in which departure, travel and arrival show themselves in their ineluctability. The migrant's dividing of the waters, imagined as birth, birth to a new life in the New World, reveals itself as death, the condition that the future proposes, the future being the very realm of utopia.

At this point, I would like to return for a moment to the uncertain etymology of the term 'exile,' or rather of the term *'ex(s)ilium.'* The hypothesis formulated by Cassiodorus, *exsolium*, puts us before a word, *solium*, which in the spectrum of meanings includes essentially two of them: throne, "seggio," and sarcophagus [fn7]. To be sure, at the point where the migrant has arrived after leaving his own land, he realizes that he has lost a "seggio" that actually he had never fully possessed, a throne that was after all so ineluctably tied to the realm of history with all the mystifications that this tie implies. The migrant is instead interested in the other meaning, which opposes itself directly to the meaning just outlined and that opens what by now is the unavoidable discourse on death, on the absence of place in the extreme point of future time, when the parabola that sprang out of the origin will reach its rest. Exile, then, places the migrant at the level of myth, places him before the universal mystery of death, before which he cannot divert himself with issues of contingency, before which he cannot divert himself at all anymore. And death as point of arrival presupposes birth as point of departure: once again it is apt to highlight that uncertainty in the writing of *ex(s)ilium*. Keeping in mind the mystery with which this etymology is surrounded and abandoning the road Cassiodorus proposed, one is still left with the term *ilium*, which is not only the Latin name of the city of Troy (and here we are reminded of another mythical journey of exile, that of Aeneas), but also means 'womb, groin,' that is, those parts of the body that are related to the function of birth. Now the term "exile" truly appears to us, in the very process of digging in search of its etymology, in equilibrium between birth and death, between the point of departure and that of arrival, in which existence continuously and ineluctably dwells. Before this last statement, the perspective of the migrant seems a privileged one for the reasons that have been listed: if migration had been forced by social and economic reasons, if history had caused the exodus, that very exodus, that journey of exiting from the place, turning upside down the expectation of the Promised Land, has placed the migrant before the truth of myth: exile is a "metaphysical condition."[3] The Promised Land is yet to come because the journey continues, and the migrant still carries the burden of his body, rescues the signs, spreads the traces of history and projects the migrant into the myth: both dimensions embrace and confuse each other in that which is "the condition we call exile."[4]

## Notes

1. Delivered at a conference organized by the Wheatland Foundation in Vienna in November 1987, the lecture was published with the title "The Condition We Call Exile, or Acorns Aweigh," in Joseph Brodsky, *On Grief and Reason: Essays*, New York: Farrar Straus and Giroux, 1995, pp.22-34; the quotation is the initial paragraph of the essay, pp. 22-23.

2. One should not dismiss the importance of the theme of exile, although seen from a different perspective, in the poetry of Pascoli: suffice to mention "Italy."

3. J. Brodsky, "The Condition We Call Exile, or Acorns Aweigh," in J. Brodsky, *On Grief and Reason: Essays*, p. 25.

4. Ibidem, p. 22.

# Ways of Writing Home

*Jim Zucchero*

THE CONNECTIONS BETWEEN HOME, IDENTITY and writing are complex and rich in meaning. Exploring the nature of these relationships has been especially important to exiles and immigrant writers, both historically and in contemporary times. Italian-Canadian writers and scholars have made important contributions to this body of writing; in fact, the thread of writing that explores relations between home and identity can be traced from the early journals of the Jesuit missionary F.G. Bressani in the seventeenth century to the poetry and stories of the latest generation of Italians to migrate to Canada and make it their home. This essay explores how several contemporary Italian-Canadian writers have worked through the relationships between home, identity and belonging, and examines some of the effects of their writing. How do these writers contribute to current discussions about home and identity? Furthermore, what does their creative work suggest about the capacity for writing to function as a tool for understanding and illuminating the complex ties between home and identity? Put another way, how have Italian-Canadian writers tried to "write their way home"?

In this instance, 'writing home' suggests the idea of articulating a dialogue between two cultures – those of Canada and Italy. This dialogue will be conceived and expressed differently by every writer because it is the product of one's unique experience, and because it is affected by so many variables: the nature of the relationship with Italy – as country of birth, or ancestral homeland; the time of migration; the age and gender of the writer, regional considerations, and so on. Writing home, then, becomes one means of trying to bridge the gap between the Italian culture of their heritage, and the Canadian culture in which they are now immersed. This essay examines very different ways of writing home: a novel, two short poems, and public discourse from the political arena. These diverse samples demonstrate that Italian-Canadian writers are constantly negotiating the relationship between their Italian cultural heritage and their Canadian cultural experience, and finding creative ways to express the dynamics of this relationship in their writing.

One question that arises is: What links these ways of writing home? Is there a common thread? If so, what does it suggest about the cultures of Italy and of Canada respectively? In each of these cases writing is a vehicle for articulating competing impulses toward nostalgia and novelty; for reconciling tensions between tradition and modernity, past and future. Writing home becomes a way to reflect upon and work through the classic immigrant dilemma of belonging to two cultures, but existing in neither one comfortably. The writing examined here resonates with much of the body of Italian-Canadian writing, and also provides insights into how it is developing in the twenty-first century.

This essay is case study in three parts: First, I discuss Mary di Michele's 2004 novel *Tenor of Love*. Next, I examine poems by two emerging Canadian poets – Capilongo and Giorno – who use humour as a key feature of their writing home. Thirdly, I consider writing by Pier Giorgio Di Cicco, a former poet laureate of Toronto who 'writes home' through his involvement in politics and civic service. Considered together, these three examples represent a diverse writing sample. But each in its own way supports my assertion that contemporary Italian-Canadian writers are producing compelling writing that makes a unique contribution to Canadian literary culture, and offers a distinctive voice in the dialogue about Canadian identity.

## Part I: Tenor of Love

In her novel *Tenor of Love* (2004), Mary di Michele gives us, first and foremost, a wonderful love story. Ideas about love are at the centre of her writing home, from Canada to Italy. *Tenor of Love* is a fictional re-creation of the life of the great Italian tenor Enrico Caruso, from the perspective of the women who loved him; namely, the sisters Ada and Rina Giachetti, and the American socialite Dorothy Benjamin Park. At another level the novel can be read as a paradigm of Italian emigration. In Caruso, the talented young Italian who comes to America to make his name, spread his art and seek his fortune, we can see the archetype of millions of Italians who would follow him and emigrate to America[1] in the twentieth century.

Consider the diverse ways in which aspects of home are represented in *Tenor of Love*. The narrative moves back and forth between Italy and America, and traces the dramatic twists and turns of Caruso's personal affairs as they unfold alongside his meteoric rise to fame and fortune. The protagonist emerges as a pack of contradictions, torn by competing impulses – his enormous ego and his self doubt; his appetite for fame and fortune and his desire for solitude and simple pleasures. Caruso was Italian to the core – in his tastes, character and disposition; and yet, he felt drawn to America. America was the land where his dreams of greatness could take flight, but Italy would forever claim his heart.

Notably, Caruso's first migration is from the South of Italy to the North – from his home in Naples to the Giachetti household in Tuscany. The young Rico is introduced as a travelling man with no pretense. When he arrives in Tuscany he is carrying his belongings in a cardboard suitcase. (10) And yet, he is a man with great dignity, entirely self-possessed, with a keen sense of his own power and presence. Above all, he displays burning ambition and supreme self-confidence. (23)

Soon after his arrival and his integration into the household, the love triangle begins to take shape. Rico is torn between the love of two sisters, Ada (the prima donna) and Rina (the innocent) – much like the immigrant whose loyalties are divided between love for the homeland and the adopted country. Perhaps not surprisingly, the naive young Caruso is taken advantage of by the impresario Goldini. His innocence and ambition make him easy prey. The parallels are hard to miss – many talented, industrious Italian immigrants in America were exploited by unscrupulous bosses, and even by some *padroni*.

When he arrives in America, Rico becomes a star almost overnight. He opens the season at the Met in New York City; soon he is being paid $5000 a night – a princely sum in 1903! (146) Like many enterprising Italian immigrants in America, Rico takes a chance and it pays off handsomely. He embraces the new recording technology and soon his voice is playing on phonographs everywhere, spreading his fame and growing his fortune. Caruso is the archetypal young entrepreneur taking big risks and collecting the benefits. But the obvious question arises: will success corrupt the young Italian star? He begins to live in great splendour during the summers at his Italian villa, *Bellosguardo*. But is he still in touch with reality and his humble roots? As if to teach him a lesson, the wheel of fortune turns: Rina and Rico have a dalliance at *Bellosguardo*, Ada bursts in, and in a fit of rage all is spoiled. (164) Now, vengeance and vindictiveness wreak havoc on their world.

Rico identifies with Italians abroad who have to roam the world to make a living, especially those in New York; but he returns to Italy each summer, to touch his native soil and to be with his two sons there. His loyalty to his cultural roots is clearly evident. Still, he can't settle on having it only one way. His loyalties and his passions are divided. While the dutiful Rina tends to his children and estate in Italy, Rico falls in love, again, this time with a shy, young American socialite named Dorothy, in New York.

Just what is it about the young American that he finds so alluring? Not so much her beauty as her innocence. She does not know him as the famous singer – Caruso. Rico is smitten by her deference; by the idea that he can mould her to his will and create with her the life he aspires to have in America. They are married, against her father's wishes, and enjoy three short years of bliss together before Caruso falls ill.

*Tenor of Love* wears its title comfortably; love is central to the novel's plot and theme, its character development and dialogue. It is all about love – lost and found, stolen and given. As in a good Italian opera, there are many racy bits: tales of betrayal, jealous sisters, a fop of a cuckold husband, bastard children – wonderful episodes that can only be mentioned in passing here. The climax of the novel comes in a passage that examines the nature of love and delivers a powerful message that bears directly on the idea of writing home.

Di Michele examines the love that binds Rico and Dorothy together; her narrator asks: "What is love and how does one choose it?" (269) Dorothy answers:

> What I believe is that love is a discovery, a synchronous discovery, made between two people. To be at home with someone – I think now that it's just that simple, and also that surprising, because that someone may be a stranger. .... with Enrico Caruso ... I found myself truly at home for the first time and with a man from the other side of the Atlantic. (269)

At the heart of the novel is the romantic idea that in love we develop to our true potential and become all we can be; that it takes a leap of faith to give oneself totally to "a stranger"; and that in bridging this great divide we grow and are made better. The story of their great love affair hints at the idea that reciprocity between the creative power of the old world (with its history and traditions) and the energy and enterprise of the new world (with its resources and opportunity) can produce a beautiful marriage – one that allows each partner to prosper and achieve his or her full humanity.

When Caruso finally succumbs to his illness and dies in his hometown of Naples, the entire city mourns his passing. It is said that he always kept his Italian citizenship, but he preferred to sing in America. In a sense, his heart was in Italy, but his bank account was in America. He needed to feed both appetites: his craving for artistic accolades, for wealth and fame, could only be sated in America. But he could not extinguish his need to be nurtured by the culture of his old home, Italy. His dilemma neatly symbolizes the divided sensibility and double loyalties of the immigrant. Despite his great success, he could never overcome his sense of being an outsider, a visitor in America.

In *Tenor of Love*, di Michele "writes home" by re-visiting and re-imagining the classic immigrant narrative in the form of a twentieth century fairytale: Caruso, the great Italian artist, makes good in America. Certain features of di Michele's novel seem typically Canadian: she strikes a perfect balance between narrative and description. She incorporates careful research of historic facts and events, but also gives us rich passages that spring from her imagination, scenes that convey deeply felt emotions of bliss and despair, anger and joy. She has written a novel of great beauty, one that engages readers as both an intimate portrait of a compelling figure, and a paradigm of Italian migration. Di Michele's love story of Caruso celebrates the possibility of bridging the great divide, but it also conveys the pain, loss and sacrifices involved in taking that big chance. It provides rich material for those interested in exploring the correspondence between the old world and the new world, between home and away. *Tenor of Love* is a sophisticated work of art from an accomplished writer – an example of the excellence of much Italian-Canadian writing released in recent years.

## Part II: Italian-Canadian Writers Find Their Funny Bone

Many of the issues of cultural disconnectedness that di Michele alludes to in *Tenor of Love* are explored with great humour by an emerging group of writers including: poets Domenico Capilongo,

Frank Giorno, Gianna Patriarca, and Giovanna Riccio, and short story writers like Marisa De Franceschi, Delia De Santis, and Bruna Di Giuseppe, to name just a few. Their humourous writing may seem simple, but it is deceptively complex. At one level, they relate comic anecdotes and humourous episodes that are entertaining in themselves. But beneath the surface their humour is provocative and instructive because it illustrates important points about social adjustment, integration, belonging and social agency. Their writing extends a long tradition of using humour as a strategy for defending against prejudice, and a tool for coping with social resistance and control. The second part of this essay examines two examples of this humourous writing and considers why humour is an effective tool for exploring relationships between Italian and Canadian cultures.

The noted Canadian media theorist Marshall McLuhan once said: "Behind every joke there is a deep cultural grievance. You cannot have a joke without a grievance." The grievance may be toward some other individual or group, or against oneself – a self-deprecating humour. In either case social dynamics are at play and very often some measure of social resistance is being expressed. Beverly Rasporich suggests that "minority humour makes an important contribution to the dialogue about Canadian identity."(53) Like McLuhan, Rasporich emphasizes the cultural elements of humour as central. She asserts: "Because humour is so deeply rooted in cultural values, attitudes and realities, it can be a highly effective means of myth-making, of telling who we are or ought to be...." (53) Capilongo and Giorno are among a new group of Italian-Canadian poets who are writing clever, funny poems that explore these questions of "who we are, or ought to be."

Their poems both share in and depart from the literary tradition from which they spring: narratives about the journey, nostalgic laments for the home left behind, and the difficulties of making enormous cultural adjustments. The titles of their publications are the first clear sign that their writing approaches traditional immigrant themes from a different perspective. Finally, sometime early in the twenty-first century, Italian-Canadian writers discovered their funny bone. In 2008 Capilongo published a collection of poems entitled *I thought elvis was italian*; that same year, Giorno released his collection of poems called *Arrivederci, Plastic-Covered Couch*. I will use the title poems from these two collections to illustrate how these two writers use humour to explore the correspondence between their Italian heritage and their experience of life in Canada, and to express their cultural grievances.

Domenico Capilongo begins his poem "I thought elvis was italian" with: "pictures of my father slick-haired & sideburned." Then he writes: "my uncles had all his albums/ ...thought he had to change his name/ like dean martin did/ the leather/ the rings & gold chains/ the way he moved his hips/ his lips/ the leather/ the sicilian black of his hair/ ...his best friend named esposito/...his fixation with cars/ the way he looked at women/ the way he put on weight/ how close he was to his mother...." (13) In his description of Elvis, Capilongo gives us a colourful list of characteristics often associated with the stereotypical Italian male. But through his opening reference to his father, his poem turns the homage to Elvis on its head. Here, homage collides with pop cultural analysis of both Elvis and Italian male stereotypes. In one fell swoop he takes on Italian male stereotypes (often held up to ridicule) and the rise and fall of perhaps the greatest American pop culture figure of the twentieth century. But it is crucial to note that his analysis of Elvis as portraying many features associated with Italian men is in the context of homage to his own father. He thought his father was like Elvis, or that Elvis was like his father: slick-haired, sideburned ... the coolest of the cool.

Capilongo's Elvis poem is at once a light-hearted bit of pop fun, and at the same time quite serious: a rejection of the mockery of Italian male strength. Just as he reveres his father's coolness (as being just like Elvis'), he recognizes that it too is temporal, fleeting and fading. Rasporich points out that "irony by minority culture writers in Canada is often directed inwards, toward immigrant realities. Typically, writers from minority culture backgrounds walk in two cultural worlds ... they are inclined to consider ... what it means to be Canadian with an ironic eye." (63) Capilongo's Elvis poem provides an excellent example of how irony and humour are being used to examine immigrant themes (in this case, ethnic stereotypes) but with a different twist; as Giovanna Riccio puts it, "the themes will persist but hopefully with new tonalities and emotions." (e-mail 30/4/10) This new humorous writing suggests to me a different level of comfort with the collective identity that has developed for Italian-Canadians, or at least a willingness to see that humour can be an effective tool for examining and exploiting the usual ethnic stereotypes. Here, the potentially hurtful barbs are in effect blunted through their being appropriated in self-deprecating humour.

Frank Giorno does something similar in his poem, "Arrivederci, Plastic-Covered Couch" but instead of a pop icon, like Elvis, he chooses an item of furniture invested with symbolic significance. The plastic-covered couch was a way of announcing to the world: "We are as good as you! We have fine furnishings too, just as nice as yours ... but we are sensible enough to secure them against all harm." In his poem, Giorno pokes fun at this idea: " 'The Arm Chair, the Love Seat, and the Holy Couch'/ We couldn't sit on them – / They were for show." (22) The plastic-covered couch is the symbol of the achievement of hard working immigrants like his parents, who "toiled in factories baking like meat in the oven" (22) while he enjoyed his first sexual encounter on the fruits of their labour. On a hot day in July, their "bodies entwined got stuck to the 'Holy Couch'/ and its sacred plastic wrap." (22) Their amorous encounter is so full of passion that it causes the furniture to break: "a crack that sounded like thunder ... a rupture ... [in their] rapture." (22)

Many years later, after his mother has died, and his widowed father has taken his last nap on it, they haul the plastic-covered couch out to the curb for garbage. Now the narrator is struck by a deep sense of sadness; tears roll down his face; he says good-bye to the plastic-covered couch as if he were burying it along with his parents. Like the Elvis poem, "Arrivederci, Plastic-Covered Couch" works at several levels. On one level there is a playful mocking tone, poking fun at the trappings of respectability. But at another level there is a serious sub-text: a reverence for family life, for hard work, sacrifice, and achievement; a sense of respect for parents that may be a thing of the past. The closing stanza conveys a deep sense of melancholy, suggesting that the death of his parents marks the passing of a generation, their culture, and their idiosyncrasies. In the end, the poem pivots on this tension between celebrating and dismissing; between recognition of virtue and the rejection of it. Giorno's clever poem inhabits the space between two generations and two continents. His narrator (like many immigrants) has a foot on each side of the great cultural divide and gazes into the abyss, uncertain which way to move. His poem underscores Rasporich's point that "irony is a defence ... a means of underlining the racial and cultural barriers of Canadian society." (63) Giorno sees his writing fitting into and extending the tradition of humourous writing by immigrants, from Chico Marx, to Louis Prima and Pat Cooper. He recognizes the various ways in which he and other Italian-Canadian writers can now use humour, sometimes turning it on themselves, at other times directing it out toward the host culture. He states: "I use humour to examine some of the absurdities and dire situations I and my contemporaries faced growing up in Toronto ... I think the shift is that we are now laughing at our own cultural standards, seeing the irony, contradictions." (e-mail 4/16/10) For Giorno, "Humour is the lubricant that allows us to live with adversity, overcome insults and injury to our pride without resorting to hostilities." (e-mail 4/16/10)

Other Italian-Canadian writers are now using humour and irony to explore the correspondence between their Italian heritage and their experience of living in Canada, and to reconcile the tensions, gaps and friction between these cultures. These writers are finding new ways of writing home and I am indebted to them for sharing their thoughts and providing much helpful input on this topic.

## Part III: Writing Home Through Public Discourse – Pier Giorgio Di Cicco

The third part of this essay considers writing by Pier Giorgio Di Cicco, an Italian-Canadian who is writing home through his political and civic involvement. Born in Arezzo, Italy in 1949, he moved to Canada in 1952 and spent his youth in Montreal, Toronto and Baltimore. He returned to Toronto and became deeply involved in the flourishing Canadian literary scene in the 1970s. A trailblazer in Italian-Canadian literature (and a founding member of the AICW), Di Cicco has published over twenty volumes of poetry. In the late 1980s he stopped publishing poetry and withdrew to a monastery. Some years later he was ordained a Catholic priest; he resumed publishing in 2001. Di Cicco served as poet laureate of Toronto from 2004 to 2009; he is said to have "extended the role beyond the area of arts advocacy and into the realm of 'civic aesthetic,' a term he coined to define building a city through citizenship, civic ethic, and urban psychology." (3) He posted a series of monographs on his web site as one means of engaging in dialogue with citizens about how to create a sustainable, stimulating city that would promote creativity and foster civility. In 2007 he published *Municipal Mind: a manifesto for the creative city*, a collection of prose writings that focus on civic engagement and the social and psychological aspects of urban life in the modern multicultural city.

Di Cicco attributes much of his strong interest in civic affairs, and his dedication to the idea of community, directly to his Italian roots. His political vision is simple but profound and consistent with his poetic disposition and Catholic faith: he asserts that we must cultivate genuine community, manifested in civility, hospitality and expressions of mutual respect for the other. In an interview given in 2004, Di Cicco credits Toronto's "pro-multicultural climate for nurturing his development as a citizen and as a poet." *(Toronto Star* (B3) 10/9/04) In personal correspondence (e-mail 2/24/04) Di Cicco wrote: "[I] saw the ethos of values at the heart of 'italianità' had to do with a metaphysic that was transubstantive and catholic ... What [I] was trying to do as a poet for a long time [was] to flesh out, to 'incarnate' the axioms of love [I] felt in the marrow of 'italianness.'"

There is a very strong correspondence between Di Cicco's political manifestos and the poetry he was writing and publishing around this time in *The Honeymoon Wilderness* (2002) and *The Dark Time of Angels* (2003). Di Cicco's pronouncements as Poet Laureate frequently reiterate his poetic musings, often using only slightly different language. He examines ideas about civility, public space and public art, creativity, and how we live together and try to make it work. He is a strong ambassador for multiculturalism, but not a zealous cheerleader for the cause who lacks critical awareness. In his postings as Poet Laureate, he offers up observations that are candid, realistic and optimistic, and analysis that is usually charitable but also incisive and sometimes distinctly edgy. The monographs and manifestos in *Municipal Mind* are, in effect, the carefully articulated reflections and prescriptions of a poet/legislator.

In fact, Di Cicco not only practices combining poetry and politics, he also preaches it as a strategy for raising people's consciousness about civic responsibility. He advocates for trying to heighten people's receptiveness to beauty in the physical world, and promotes the idea that such a "poetic" sensitivity should translate into an increased sense of civic pride and engagement.

In his inaugural speech as Poet Laureate (on September 29, 2004), he explained how poetry could play an integral role in helping the citizens of Toronto to enhance the quality of their civic interactions. He stated:

> Poetry is not something sitting on a page. It is a way of life, a way of being, a way of interacting that sometimes finds its expression on the page; and the pages of poetry may teach people how to live poetically, or more precisely, with passion ... Passion is about taking risks in any sector of endeavour, for the good of many and for the elevation of the human spirit. And passion is the way we encourage each other to those ends. Poetry is the record of that passion and the rallying cry for that passion.

Di Cicco has written about trust as "a civic resource" and says cities must be attentive to how this trust is eroded and eventually negated by the imposition of certain kinds of policies, bylaws and procedures. As Poet Laureate he examines the idea of faith, not in the religious sense but rather in a secular sense, as an indispensable public virtue. He develops the idea that secular faith is akin to religious faith in that both have to be cultivated – believed in and hoped for. One direct consequence of this notion of civic faith is that we create and are responsible for the world we inhabit, and for each other, personally and socially. This is an example of Di Cicco's transposing principles from his religious life into the civic arena.

Di Cicco is a compelling figure and one who has made a significant contribution to Italian-Canadian literature, and to Canadian political life, especially in Toronto. His engagement in civic life clearly demonstrates his commitment to the values of Canadian multiculturalism, but it also speaks to the deep influence of his Italian cultural heritage, something he feels in the very marrow of his bones. His writing – both his poetry and his political manifestos – provides clear evidence that he has found different creative outlets for working through the competing and complementary cultural influences that constitute his identity.

In conclusion, the examples that I have cited here, from di Michele's novel, *Tenor of Love*, to the humourous poetry of Capilongo and Giorno, and to the political pronouncements of Di Cicco, demonstrate that Italian-Canadians are continuously re-inventing ways of writing home. They are finding creative ways of exploring and expressing the rapport between these two great cultures and nations. This writing makes a unique and important contribution to the development of Canadian identity; it also reminds us of the challenges and the rewards experienced by those who share and try to bridge the lived experience of these two cultural worlds.

## Note

1. In the early twentieth century the concept of 'America' in the Italian immigrant imagination largely collapsed national distinctions between the USA and Canada, and even South America and other destinations such as Australia. This point is noted in much of the literature on Italian migration, including an article by S. Iuliano and L. Baldassar who state: "... for millions of actual emigrants from the Italian peninsula in the nineteenth and twentieth centuries, "l'America" was as much a state of mind as a place. It encompassed all places overseas that held out the promise of wealth and security ..."

## Works Cited

Capilongo, Domenico. *I thought elvis was italian*. Hamilton: Wolsak and Wynn, 2008.

Di Cicco, Pier Giorgio. *Municipal Mind: manifestos for the creative city*. Toronto: Mansfield, 2007.

_____. *The Dark Time of Angels*. Toronto: Mansfield, 2003.

_____. *The Honeymoon Wilderness*. Toronto: Mansfield, 2002.

Di Michele, Mary. *Tenor of Love*. Toronto: Penguin, 2004.

Giorno, Frank. *Arrivederci, Plastic-Covered Couch*. Toronto: Lyricalmyrical, 2008.

Iuliano, Susanna, and Loretta Baldassar, "Deprovincialising Italian Migration Studies" in Flinders University Languages Group Online Review, Volume 3, Issue 3, Nov. 2008.

McLuhan, Marshall. In *Quotable Canada – a national treasury*. Ed. John Robert Colombo. New York: Running Press, 1998.

Rasporich, Beverly. "Canadian Humour and National Culture." *Canadian Cultural Poesis: Essays on Canadian Culture*. Eds. Garry Sherbert, Annie Gérin, and Sheila Petty. Waterloo (ON): Wilfrid Laurier UP, 2006, 51-66.

# Part II

# Creative Visitations
*Voicing Old and New Homes*

# Entering Sicily[1]

### *Darlene Madott*

SOON AFTER WE ENTER SICILY, my grandmother's story begins to inform what I see. I stare out the window at the slopes of hills as sensuous as the breasts of reclining women, hills planted at perilous inclines, with modern windmills now cresting these – not Nicolina Leone's Sicily, at all. But I intuit from the walled estates, the outcropped single room dwellings which still offer respite from the midday sun, what it must have been to be the daughter of a *padrone*, the husbandman who oversaw the owner's lands and labourers, in the absence of the titled owner in Palermo or Messina.

"I can still see my father's house," Nicolina said, the last time I saw her alive. She was feeling blindly for her piece of chicken on the plate. It would be my last visit with her and the aged aunt in whose home she then lived. Nicolina stared into the distance behind memory. "I see my father's house…"

What my grandmother described of her father's house was of the young woman she must have been, once, serving food and wine with her stepmother, to the second storey, where only the men would eat at the long table.

"My lips never touched the glass."

"Well, you're never too old to learn," I said. Astonishingly, my grandmother smiled and took a sip from the shot glass of wine I insisted on pouring for her and placing in her hand. She was one hundred and three. That day she ate with appetite.

"You don't take photographs here, and you don't ask questions about Leones, Spataforas, or anybody else," Warren advises.

We are in Salemi – sister town to Vita, in Sicily. Warren has driven us out from Palermo, and we arrive in Salemi about 10:30 a.m. We head to a bar just off what seems to be the main square, and I order *panini* and *due espressi*, mindful of the time, to make it to Vita before the siesta.

"Do you think we stick out?" Warren asks, being facetious.

He is wearing a Red Wings' hockey jacket from Canada and is of a weight and presence that towers above the diminutive men in the bar. I wear a brown leather jacket and blue jeans with zippered pockets. But it is more than our clothing. I am the only woman at the bar. And we speak to each other, in English. We are *stranieri*.

As we eat our *panini*, the old men of Salemi stare at us, and we look back at them, looking back at us. Staring is an Italian sport.

According to her own story, no one had ever loved Nicolina as much as her stepmother; nor had she ever loved another as much as that good woman. It wasn't always so. The adored apple of her father's eye, Nicolina looked upon the stepmother as usurper of her father's attentions. Nicolina was only three when her mother died falling off a horse with the unborn twins twisted in her womb, when her father re-married. Initially, Nicolina would have none of the stepmother, gave her a tough time. Until the day the stepmother placed her firmly in a tub of water, and gave her a bath. While administering to Nicolina's body, in soap and water to the elbows and on her knees, she made a deal with her three-year-old stepdaughter.

*Your father will always prefer you to me, but he needs me to help him take care of you. This can either work well for us both, or it can go really hard. It's your choice. Respect me, and I will love you, always. But if you choose to go against me, it will go very badly for us both. The choice is yours.*

How did she figure it out, in those days before psychologists, to position it thus before a rebellious, fiercely intelligent and manipulative three-year-old – to give Nicolina the choice?

"Think of the times," I say to Warren, "what it must have been – a woman alone. You either married or you starved, and what a dangerous business it must have been in those days, keeping the love of a tough man."

"That tastes good," says Warren to the owner of the bakery we have entered in Salemi, to get directions to the sister town of Vita. The slender owner, comprehending, laughs with her mouth stuffed full of *cannoli*, and signals with her free hand toward her shelves, palm outstretched and welcoming, as if to say, *please, help yourselves*. While Warren delights his eyes with the fresh pastries, I am fascinated by the sculpted and lacquered breads in varying designs. I purchase two clusters of bread grapes – one for my mother back in Canada, one for my own harvest table.

*Nicolina sings to me, clapping the hands of my then infant son…*

*Batti manini ca veni Papà*
*porta cose e sinni va*
*porta nuci e cassateddi*
*pi manciari ai figghi beddi.*
      *Porta mennuli e castagni*
      *Pi accurdari a chiddi granni.*
*Here comes Papa, so clap these hands*
*He brings good things, all from the land;*
*He brings you nuts and little cakes,*
*Melons and fruit to make you great.*
      *Almonds and chestnuts, sweet cheese for this day*
      *A kiss for Mama, and then he's away.*

"My little Vito," keened Nicolina, "I see my Vito…"

*Don't say it, I think, don't tell me that story, not while holding the hands of my own infant son …*

"He used to run to me, and pound his little chest. I gave him life. I could not give him breath."

"My great-grandfather had to be tough, or he would have starved. They all would have starved along with him." And Nicolina's father was tougher than most – a *padrone* of another's lands.

The stepmother, herself widowed, came to the marriage with a son, Paolo, with whom Nicolina later fell in love when her time came to discover love. Her father forbade this love, married her instead to the Spatafora who would eventually take her to Canada –breaking three hearts in the process – four, if you included his own.

From the hilltop town of Salemi, I see a vineyard of *Nero d'Avola* grapes, and wonder if this might have been part of the very lands my great-grandfather oversaw?

I must have heard it at my aunt's table – the aunt who was taking care of my aged grandmother. My grandmother was only sixteen at the time when my great-grandfather forced her to marry the man who would become my grandfather – Rosario Spatafora. In those days, when a man wept for weeks without explanation, he was put into a mental institution. Nicolina had to wait until she was of legal age, before she could sign him out – her sensitive young husband – the man who had crossed the ocean four times, the man her father had forced her to marry. Rosario's fifth crossing would be his last – with Nicolina, then twenty-one. He would never return again.

"Yolked to a sick man... On my wedding night they gave me a bowl of water and vinegar, with a cloth. *O Dio,* married to a sick man..."

"Why didn't you tell me that my grandfather had a nervous breakdown?" I challenge my mother, when I first learn of my grandfather's incarceration in a mental institution.

"What difference would it have made?"

"It would have helped explain."

"Explain what?"

Explain why Nicolina had no children, the first five years of her marriage, why they all came afterward – in Canada. Explain me, possibly, to myself. Explain that motion sickness of the soul, what happens when you lose your centre of gravity, travel too many distances too many times, too far from home – the unbearable suffering of the displaced person. Explain how I myself had felt, after Vancouver, the panic attacks – the most recent of these in Agrigento, in the *Valle dei Templi* – as Warren slept through the siesta and I clung to his breathing body, as if to *home*.

"So when the guys back at the coffee shop ask me how I spent my vacation, I'll tell them I wandered around graveyards." The coffee shop to which my Warren refers is Messina Bakery in Toronto. The coffee shop in Salemi was called Extra Bar.

The names: Spatafora, Leone, Agueci, Caradonna, Gandolfo, Pedone, Boscaglia, Gucciardi, Pace – vaguely familiar – names heard in my parents' stories of growing up around Clinton and College, in Toronto.

Spatafora. Of those who remained, they must have done all right for themselves, because there is a Spatafora mausoleum, in the newest part of the Vita graveyard.

None of the graves are old enough to be recognized by my parents as contemporaries of Nicolina, though the names are shared. She arrived in Canada just at the turn of the century, in 1906. Still, I take pictures.

GUCCIARDI MARIA　　SPATAFORA MICHELE
VED. SPATAFORA　　　FU GIUSEPPE
*26-9-1881 + 2-12-1974　　*25-10-1872 + 14-9-1958

Nicolina Leone returned to Vita in Sicily only once, for the death and burial of her father. She stayed almost a year, accompanied by her two small children, infants under five. She returned to keep vigil over her dying father and then, upon his death, remained for some time longer to be of comfort to her stepmother. And when Nicolina left Vita that final time – after having seen her father honoured with the tomb built with the money she had inherited from him – she left in a *carretto tirato da un cavallo*, her stepmother walk-running at the wagon's side. For miles, the stepmother accompanied them on foot. And Nicolina would stop the driver and get down and embrace the old woman, and the old woman would embrace Nicolina and the children she was certain never to see again. And for as many miles as Nicolina could bear, it went on like this, with the old woman beside the cart, weeping, and the cart stopping and everyone getting out, embracing, weeping, and back in again – struggling to say goodbye in a way the adult women knew to be final. Until at last, the old woman stood still in the dusty road and watched, as they passed out of sight on the road *direzione* Palermo, from there to Naples, to the boat that would take them across the ocean, forever.

*Forever. Never again. Not ever, in this lifetime. How do you do that – part – when you know you will never, ever, see the object of your love, again?*

"How many churches can there be in a town this size?"

The one church I am seeking – the one where my grandmother caused to have a plaque made in honour of her father's memory, I cannot find. It was probably bombed during the war, or lost in an earthquake. The only church we do find, and this before the siesta, is closed. The founding dates on the plaque outside its central door are beyond the dates of my grandmother's story.

"She was running after her nephew," my mother says. "I think her name was Anna, my real grandmother, the one who died, falling from a horse."

"What do you mean, *running after*?"

My mother explains: "Her husband's brother had a son, Vito. I guess he was a young boy, and his father used to beat him. They were tough customers, in those days."

"Who, my great-grandfather?"

"No, his brother. But they were both tough customers. Vito ran away. Your great-grandmother, Anna, I think her name was, she got on a horse and chased after him, to bring him home. But she was pregnant, and fell off the horse, and that's how she died."

The town of Vita feels dead. It is more alive in the graveyard, above the town, where at least there are the pictures of its former inhabitants. With its rows of mausoleums, the Vita graveyard mimics the society of the town below, but on a miniature scale. And what hard faces stare out of these stones – as if not a single life had been happy.

Survivors of Vita Bascaglia have planted roses. Three buds burst pink, red and salmon to adorn her tombstone – monument of a life lived from 1898 to 1973. I think of the profusion of roses that bloomed around Nicolina's porch – the scent of summer so heady I'd feel drunk on my tea and my grandmother's porch stories.

"I do not feel her spirit here," I say to Warren. "She has gone from this place, entirely. My cousin said she felt Nicolina here. She found the town closed, and also came to a graveyard. She said she felt our grandmother's spirit. I feel nothing."

"Did you expect your grandmother to hang around in a place like this forever?"

I have told him, of course, the story of Nicolina's death – how the aged aunt took my grandmother and herself to an old folks' home. The aunt stayed in the assisted living wing, while my grandmother was put in with the really decrepit – those with dementia and Alzheimer's, and those who couldn't "do for themselves." Nicolina, although blind and deaf, had all her mental faculties. She protested in not-so-subtle ways. "*Perché sono qui?*" "Why am I here?" she would proclaim at the dinner table, where her dinner companions were strapped to their wheelchairs and stared, disinterested, at their Canadian food. Ever an elegant woman, whose father had returned from Palermo with parasols and bolts of fabric she turned into the fashions of the day, Nicolina would break wind at this last dinner table, to lend emphasis to her protest. There was no one here with whom to make a deal. At night, she called out names – of those she had loved, or who had loved her. Sadly, my mother's name was not among them.

Three days before she died, Nicolina had her last bowel movement. She washed her private parts – never permitting anyone to touch these. She lay on her bed, and folded her hands neatly across her chest. She summoned Aunt Vitina to shave her – Vitina, named after the town and the dead little boy, Vito, who had come and gone before her. Nicolina willed her own death. The vanity with which she had lived her life ensured her face would be hairless in its final display. In fact, Nicolina had looked resplendent in death.

"Don't worry," Warren says to me, in the car, just outside the graveyard of Vita. "I will find someone to shave you."

"Forget the shave. It's about the picture on my grave..."

Tough. They were all tough – tough as in hanging two loads of laundry while in labour with your first child.

Tough, as in being forced to marry your father's choice.

Tough, as in burying your child – named after a town in Sicily that means "life."

Tough, as in pretending not to recognize your youngest child, my mother, your daughter, while she was washing your face during those final three days – "Francesca? Who?" When you well knew who she was – lucid to the last moment. Because love did not exist in your vocabulary, then, not ever again, after your tough father married you to the Spatafora who took you to Canada, not ever again after your stepmother died.

*Forever. Never again. Not ever, in this lifetime. How do you do that – part – when you know you will never, ever, see the object of your love, again?*

"Ma, if it came to a choice between hearing it from my mother and hearing it from my own child, I'd rather hear it from my child" – words I said to my mother after Nicolina's death, when my mother could not get over her grief, that Nicolina had died without acknowledging her – whose hand it was that held the wash cloth: "I love you, Ma, I love you."

Vito. Vita. Vitina.

Names on stones. Lifetimes reduced to a single story line: "Anna, I think her name was. She died falling off a horse, the unborn twins twisted in her womb." Names on stones. Names, ultimately, that identify nothing – a slow relentless vanishing...

"Take a picture," Warren says, as we leave Vita. Obediently, I turn around in the car, and stick my camera out the window, backwards. The sign is rusted, and bears the symbol for "no horns." The sign says:

VITA
BENVENUTI A
WELCOME TO
BIENVENUE A
WILLKOMMEN IN
VITA

I make my Warren toot the horn, in defiance and affirmation. As always, he obliges me. He has no idea why I ask him to honk it, looks at me, surprised and uncomprehending. Yes, blow it – again – hard. Lean on that horn! Sound the horn for those who can no longer hear it. Yes, sound it, for me.

## Note

1. This is the version read at the Atri conference. "Entering Sicily" also appears in Darlene Madott's collection *Stations of the Heart* (Exile Editions, 2012) and in *Descant 154: Sicily, Land of Forgotten Dreams*, Vol. 42, No. 3, Fall 2011.

# Pastafasù

## Nino Famà

*(estratto da un romanzo ancora in lavorazione)*

NEGLI ULTIMI TEMPI DON PEPPINO camminava per le strade di Brooklyn distratto, soprappensiero. Era talmente sbadato che non si accorgeva se qualche amico lo salutava o se attraversava la strada col semaforo rosso. Provava un profondo senso d'angoscia, di smarrimento; aveva l'aria trasognata, sembrava uno smemorato. Usciva di casa per liberarsi la mente dai pensieri che lo opprimevano.

Cadeva facilmente nella disperazione quando tirava le somme della sua vita in questo paese. Le sue decisioni erano sempre state guidate da chiarezza e semplicità; non aveva mai coltivato vaghe illusioni o aspirazioni velleitarie. Era sempre stato un uomo pragmatico, non cercava la ricchezza, auspicava per la sua famiglia una vita modesta, ma comoda e dignitosa. Aveva avuto tanti dubbi, aveva fatto mille ragionamenti prima di lasciare la sua terra, ma alla fine aveva deciso di partire per poter creare le condizioni per mettere su famiglia, senza il cruccio di non poter provvedere debitamente.

Era partito con idee chiare ed obiettivi ben precisi. Si era sposato qualche anno dopo con Rosalia ed ora avevano tre figli, due maschi e una femmina. Secondo il modo di ragionare di questo paese questo costituiva il numero ideale, tre figli e un cane. A don Peppino mancava il cane. Ma non tutto si era avverato come lui l'aveva immaginato prima di lasciare la sua terra. Aveva sempre sognato una famiglia esemplare, figli obbedienti che avrebbero studiato e avrebbero intrapreso una professione: medico, avvocato, anche maestro sarebbe stato accettabile. Invece, tutto sembrava andare in direzione opposta. Don Peppino si era quasi preso un esaurimento con Pastafasù, il suo primogenito. Questi era un ragazzo ostinato, cocciuto, aveva una testa dura come un macigno ed aveva sempre protestato vigorosamente quando i genitori gli consigliavano di fare questa o quell'altra cosa.

Per la scuola Pastafasù aveva sempre provato la massima avversione. Era pigro, indolente, l'incubo dei maestri. Sin da bambino, era stato indisciplinato, disobbediente e ribelle. Non erano bastati gli incitamenti del padre né gli incoraggiamenti della madre; Pastafasù di scuola non ne voleva proprio sapere. Don Peppino a volte perdeva la pazienza e gli dava qualche sculacciata. Quando il ragazzo chiamò la polizia, come aveva imparato a scuola di fare in questi casi, per un pelo don Peppino non andò a finire in galera. I maestri, quando non ne potevano più, facevano venire i genitori a scuola, li interpellavano, spiegavano loro la situazione, ma le cose continuavano sempre uguali. I genitori si scervellavano, impazzivano, ma non vi era soluzione che reggesse; il ragazzo sembrava più intemperante che mai e dimostrava sempre più ripugnanza per la scuola. Il sistema non tollerava le bocciature e Pastafasù arrivò alle medie e conseguì il diploma: "per fare il somaro," rimbrottava don Peppino quando si arrabbiava.

Alle medie, il ragazzo ormai adolescente, incominciò a frequentare nuovi amici e con loro andava a feste e *party* dove si faceva abbondante uso di alcol e di stupefacenti. Inutili furono le esortazioni della madre e le frequenti preghiere che lei offriva a Santa Rosalia. Il ragazzo aveva imboccato una strada che faceva disperare i genitori. Don Peppino era diventato un pugno di nervi, parlava poco, ma quando esplodeva, svuotava il sacco. Nel suo cuore sapeva che le sue folate di rabbia non avrebbero risolto nulla, non sarebbero servite a facilitare una riconciliazione, un ravvicinamento tra padre e figlio. Era solo un modo per liberarsi dalla rabbia, dal rovello che logorava la sua esistenza. Rosalia gli ripeteva spesso che era un uomo dalla forte corazza esterna, ma con il cuore di ricotta. Don Peppino ricordava come ai suoi tempi, cioè quando lui aveva quell'età, le cose erano diverse. Doveva lavorare nelle campagne tutta la giornata e poi, la sera, quando tornava a casa, non gli rimaneva l'energia per fare il ribelle. E poi, se suo padre diceva una cosa, era così e basta, niente argomenti, discussioni, proteste. Rosalia spesso gli ricordava che, nonostante il loro calvario, non aveva nessun desiderio di tornare a quei tempi antichi.

"Ci vogliono disciplina, ordine, ubbidienza; cose che mancano ai ragazzi d'oggi. Troppa libertà e la legge che li protegge; devi rimanere zitto se non vuoi andare a finire dietro le sbarre," borbottava don Peppino.

"Vedrai che tutto passerà," rispondeva Rosalia per incoraggiarlo, ma lui non vedeva come, una volta scivolati nel fango, i ragazzi ne potessero venir fuori. L'atteggiamento di questo suo figlio non lasciava sperare troppo. Le cose andavano di male in peggio. Avrebbe voluto sbarrare la porta e lasciare il ragazzo fuori. Voleva proprio svincolarsi dalle responsabilità di genitore, "Così imparerà una buona lezione," brontolava a sua moglie, ma sapeva che lei non gliel'avrebbe mai permesso. E poi, essendo il ragazzo ancora giovane, il padre sarebbe andato a finire in galera per abbandono di minori. L'amarezza non gli permetteva di perdonare. Non poteva cancellare dalla sua mente quella notte in cui lo chiamò la polizia, avvertendolo che suo figlio era stato trattenuto in caserma, perché in possesso di stupefacenti. Il padre era rimasto immobile, stordito. Era andata Rosalia a firmare e a riportarsi il figlio a casa.

Pastafasù era stato la pecora nera della famiglia; colui che aveva imboccato un cammino sbagliato, che aveva deluso don Peppino il quale aveva sempre creduto di essere emigrato per creare un futuro prospero e tranquillo per i propri figli. Così l'aveva immaginato prima di partire. La delusione aveva messo a soqquadro le forze e l'animo del genitore. Don Peppino aveva raggiunto la disperazione, ma si era rassegnato ed aveva puntato le sue speranze sugli altri due figli. Sicuramente Teresa che era cresciuta legata alla madre non avrebbe causato simili guai alla famiglia, pensò. Franky era talmente ossessionato dal gioco del pallone da non aver tempo per pensare ad altro. Aveva incominciato a guardare le partite la domenica assieme al padre il quale, in patria, non si era mai interessato di calcio, ma arrivato in questo paese lo guardava ogni domenica in televisione, non perché apprezzasse il gioco in sé, ma perché era diventato un rito, lo faceva sentire più vicino alla sua terra. Franky aveva incominciato così, guardando le partite con il padre, e poi aveva iniziato a giocare con le squadre della scuola ed era arrivato a far parte di una squadra giovanile.

Man mano che passarono gli anni, sorprendentemente, Pastafasù incominciò a dimostrare che qualcosa stesse cambiando in lui. Il figlio, ora ventunenne, continuava ad essere indisciplinato e disubbidiente, ma incominciava a dimostrare la volontà di sedersi con i genitori e discutere, fare dei ragionamenti, anche se alla fine faceva sempre di testa sua. Era puntuale ed operoso nel suo lavoro di *pizza delivery*, ma non era riuscito ad abbandonare totalmente l'uso di stupefacenti. Se i genitori dimostravano diffidenza e opposizione alle sue scelte, lui rispondeva che le sostanze delle quali faceva uso, erano molto meno nocive del fumo delle sigarette. Don Peppino non era del tutto convinto, ma dopo anni di zuffe questo sembrava un nuovo inizio, un buon auspicio e sperava che prima o poi il resto arrivasse da sé. Era disposto ad aspettare, a lasciare tutto nelle mani del buon Dio.

Il fatto che Teresa avesse scelto di frequentare la Yale University a New Haven nel Connecticut, e non una delle università di New York, aveva scosso i nervi di Rosalia. Yale distava il sufficiente da Brooklyn per scoraggiare don Peppino a raggiungerla in macchina. Questo atteggiamento era stato qualcosa di estenuante per la madre. In questo paese era cosa ben accettata che arrivati all'età di frequentare l'università, molti giovani preferivano allontanarsi da casa, essere indipendenti, autonomi, autosufficienti. Infatti, era molto comune che i giovani andassero via da casa, come gli uccelli che volano via dal nido. Non era niente d'eccezionale e non doveva allarmare nessuno; faceva parte della vita, del passaggio rituale da giovani dipendenti ad adulti emancipati. Questo, Rosalia l'aveva sempre capito, queste erano le usanze, le tradizioni di questo paese. In verità le era toccato spesso dover consolare e rassicurare qualche amica la cui figlia era andata via da casa. Rosalia possedeva una certa disposizione naturale per confortare e rasserenare le amiche, convincerle che si trattava di qualcosa del tutto normale.

Fu tutta un'altra cosa, però, quando Teresa prese quella decisione. Rosalia era rimasta di stucco; non vi era ragione, non vi era argomento che potesse attutire la sua angoscia. Si trattava di una reazione che non sapeva spiegarsi, di un'emozione che non sapeva definire. Questa era la sua bambina. Non poteva essere vero che all'improvviso potesse andarsene, separarsi dalla madre che l'aveva allattata, l'aveva vista crescere e spampanare come una rosa nel mese di maggio. Forse non era vero, stava immaginando tutto, si trattava solo d'un brutto sogno.

Don Peppino si era chiuso nel silenzio. Non parlava con nessuno, nemmeno con Rosalia. Ogni tanto usciva di casa, così, per scacciare i diavoli dalla testa. Per le strade non vedeva nessuno, non salutava nessuno, non entrava nei bar o nei circoli paesani per farsi una partita a briscola, a tressette o prendere un caffè. "Il caffè gli avrebbe dato ai nervi," pensava. Si accontentava di camminare, fare delle lunghe passeggiate senza una meta precisa. Camminava ininterrottamente, giungendo fino alla zona residenziale dove abitavano gli ebrei ortodossi, quelli che portano vestiti neri ed il cappello a larghe falde. Sapeva che qui non l'avrebbe riconosciuto nessuno e avrebbe potuto camminare tranquillo, per i fatti suoi. E così faceva, giorno dopo giorno, come un sonnambulo, si dimenava per quelle strade residenziali, confuso, disorientato, frastornato. Cercava di dare ordine ai suoi pensieri, voleva dare un senso alle vicende che in questi ultimi tempi lo avevano rintronato. Il fatto che Teresa avesse preferito andarsene lontano l'aveva sconvolto, ma la notizia che fosse andata a convivere con il suo ragazzo l'aveva spinto sull'orlo del precipizio. Cercava nella sua testa una spiegazione, una giustificazione. Forse veniva castigato dal Padreterno per qualche suo oltraggio. Non sapeva proprio dare un senso a ciò che era accaduto. Si costernava, la sua mente lo riportava ad una realtà anteriore alla sua partenza e solo lì, in quell'angolo remoto della sua mente, ritrovava l'ordine che disperatamente agognava. Era l'antidoto al presente, al caos, all'incubo che i suoi figli gli stavano facendo vivere. Cercava le risposte, la soluzione, nell'ordine di quell'angolo di mondo che lui aveva abbandonato tantissimi anni addietro per andare alla ricerca di una vita migliore. "Tutto il contrario mi è capitato," ripeteva tra sé. Ogni tanto sentiva dire che il mondo era cambiato, la stessa realtà era presente ovunque si andasse. "Tutto il mondo è paese," diceva qualche amico che di recente si era recato al paese natio per fare una visita. Don Peppino rimaneva scettico, non credeva che quel luogo la cui immagine rimaneva incastonata nella sua mente come una pietra fosse potuto cambiare.

In casa, gli eventi di questi ultimi tempi avevano dato luogo ad una certa tensione, il nervosismo era nell'aria, il disappunto che i genitori provavano per la condotta dei figli spesso era come una nebbia nera discesa sulla loro casa. Rosalia, inizialmente aveva provato rabbia, si era sentita tradita, aveva visto tutti i suoi sacrifici evaporarsi in un attimo. La sua vita aveva trovato senso e giustificazione nei figli; ora si sentiva defraudata, sola. Ma Rosalia non si fece travolgere dalle emozioni. Passati i giorni di furore, ragionò fra sé e adottò un atteggiamento assai più pragmatico. Pensò che la disperazione e l'angoscia non avrebbero risolto nulla e quindi si rassegnò ed incominciò a congetturare. Cercò nuove configurazioni, nuovi allineamenti; cercò di dare un nuovo senso alla situazione, dei nuovi contesti psicologici e sociali nei costumi di questa società, cercò di trovare una nuova percezione delle cose. Per la prima volta cercò di tenere per sé i consigli che spesse volte aveva ritenuto opportuni solo per gli altri, soprattutto cercò di venirne fuori con una nuova coscienza. "Non è la fine del mondo," disse a suo marito che stava seduto accanto a lei, nella sua poltrona. Lui non rispose.

# Two Poems

*Venera Fazio*

### Invocation

My grandmother is the viper
in the family nest.
Her venom pierces generations
is potent in stories of
glacial blue eyes
velocity of temper and
as a perpetrator of grudges.

*Nonna* Venera
is the cautionary namesake I invoke
when ever I am tempted
to strike.

## The Elixir of Bafia, Sicily

*After reading Maria Famà's "The Elixir of Pietra Rimita"*

Each day of my vacation
in the village of my birth
I drew elixir from the well
in the central square.

Cup after cup tasted
cool pure light delectable delicious
intoxicating
infinitely more satisfying than
Canadian tap water
Perrier Pellegrino Aquafina.

My body rejoiced recognizing
the same life essence
shared communion with
generations of ancestors.

# The Funeral[1]

*Osvaldo Zappa*

THE SUN WAS HIGH ABOVE us when we finally came out of the shop and set off along the stony path still caked with cow dung. Stables and haylofts lined the way. There was an eerie quietness in the square, now empty of people. With the exception of stray dogs, only Rosa's hog ventured outdoors in the heat. Rosa would let the pig out to wallow in the mud from the fountain's run-off, where it would lie on its side snorting away. Despite the stables, the air smelled of drying hay and wild juniper from the surrounding hills and the wild mint from the fields and small garden plots. Like two thieves smuggling booty out of town, we carried the casket to the house some distance away.

When we reached the house, two men, both dressed in black wool suits, were already there waiting for us. My uncle and I put down the empty casket, greeted the two men and, turning to me, uncle signalled for me to wait outside while he and the others entered the squalid hut. I was relieved that I did not have to enter that house and watch them put the body in the coffin. I feared getting more lice on me. Taking measurements of the deceased was one thing but, having to lift up the poor soul infested with lice, oh, no, I wanted none of that! I would much rather stay outside. From just outside the doorway I could hear the old lady's mournful sobs. Until now I did not think the old woman capable of crying. Perhaps for the first time she understood that her dear companion was gone.

The task to move the body to the lower floor proved to be challenging for the three men. Because of the steep angle of the wooden stairs and the restricted opening of the trap door into the room, the men resorted to tying ropes around the heavy coffin. Then holding on to the ropes from above, they slowly lowered the casket while my uncle guided it down the steps until it reached the floor below.

As I waited I was distracted by the swallows building clay nests under the eaves of the old house just above the small window of the upstairs bedroom where the old man died. The temptation was too great to resist. Often my classmates and I would see who could hit these nests first with our slingshots. I gathered a few small stones for my weapon, which I often kept in the pocket of my shorts, and began shooting at the nests. I considered myself a pretty good shot of sorts. Sooner or later I was sure I would hit one. After trying a few times with the slingshot and missing, I switched to throwing larger stones. Then I picked up a shard of a roofing tile that seemed just right and hurled it with all my childish might towards one of the nests. *Voilà*, bull's eye!

A handful of dirt cascaded down, mostly on my head. Looking down at my feet I noticed a small pile of feathers and caked mud as well as two whitish, featherless little chicks, stunned from the fall. Gently I picked one up. It was still moving but was too young to fly away or to keep. I put it down beside the other one that lay very still. It was dead. In a vain attempt to protect their young, two very angry swallows zoomed down on me, spoiling my small victory. Then a rather strange feeling of guilt came over me. Feeling foolish and stupid, I picked up the live chick and in an attempt to set it free, I hurled it on the roof of a low lying shed on the opposite side of the old woman's house. The little bird landed, albeit, with a thud. A tingling breeze touched my face. I thought I felt the tip of an angry swift's wing, as if in retribution for my cowardly act. In my right hand tiny drops of blood were already drying up.

Two more men, also dressed in black, soon arrived on the scene. They also waited by the door. While they waited, Don Francesco, the priest in his black cassock, appeared at the top of the cobbled street. He seemed in a hurry and determined while a young boy behind him struggled to keep pace. As soon as he reached the house, the midday lull was broken by the slow and rhythmic knell of the church bell, which, however, displaced dozens of pigeons lodging in the rafters of the bell tower. A whole swarm of them, flying in formation, swooped down on rooftops cutting the morning sky like razors. The tolling of the bell summoned the villagers to the funeral of one of their own.

Three elderly women in long black dresses, their heads covered in white headscarves and hands folded, arrived to join in the funeral procession as the four scrawny men bronzed by the sun, the boy in shorts and the priest in black entered the house. I remained outside looking in through a small window.

The priest put on a white chasuble and draped a black sash around his neck. Beside him, the boy held a candle in one hand and holy water in the other. The priest hurried through the short prayers, sprinkling holy water on the dead man in the open coffin. Later uncle said there were many lice moving all over the dead man's black suit.

Soon after my uncle partly nailed the coffin down and the men carried it outside. The priest then read from the prayer book and the men heaved the coffin to their shoulders and started their slow march to the burial site. Two steps behind the priest the boy followed with the holy water and behind him the old women. Wearing our black armbands, uncle and I formed the rear of the cortege. Too frail and still too much in shock to follow, the widow stayed behind. Proceeding slowly, the priest recited verses from the lectionary, to which the women responded monotonously: "Santa Maria ora pro nobis…" Here the boy stepped in front of the priest, swinging the incense-burning *turibolo* like a pendulum, sending up a small plume of white smoke. The heat was stifling and the flies persistent under the hot blue sky.

On the way to the cemetery, along the street that smelled of the stables, only a handful of people came out to pay their last respects to the dead man. It was customary at that time to request, for a small fee payable to the priest, that the casket be set down in front of peoples' homes along the way in memory of the dead and out of respect for the family. In this case there were no requests so the small cortege proceeded directly to the cemetery. My uncle, still wearing paint and glue-stained overalls and carrying a hammer and screwdriver in his side strap, kept behind at a slower pace and I still slower. This was, on my part, a futile attempt to distance myself from the funeral procession, to be seen only as the carpenter's helper.

A strange scraggy stray dog appeared out of nowhere and joined the funeral cortege, walking by my side and stubbornly refusing to move away. "Maybe it belongs to the dead man," I thought. It is said that a pet senses the loss of its master and reacts in almost human fashion to this. But with the dog and the dung-smells, there were flies buzzing around.

"Gee," I thought, "this dog really wants to pay his last respects to his master!" Nevertheless, I tried shooing it away. It wouldn't go, so I resorted to kicking it, trying to force it away. Nothing seemed to work. My uncle had to grab me by the scruff of the neck to bring me back to the solemnity of the affair.

When we passed the school, the children were still in the classrooms. Appearing from behind the shuttered windows that had been left ajar because of the heat, my schoolmates were jostling for a better view. They probably envied me for missing class that day and for walking in the cortege. For children, any cortege or procession, be it happy or sad, is a sort of a parade and a cheerful event.

Along the way, here and there, windows adorned with black draperies were left open as a reverent farewell to the dead man. Women appeared momentarily, sad faced, crossing themselves but soon withdrawing into the shadows of their houses. Meanwhile, the heavy bell continued tolling loudly and steadily, reverberating in the warm and gentle breeze, reminding us all of man's brief time here on earth. Within hearing, workers in the fields put down their farming implements, paused, made the sign of the cross and then resumed their tasks.

A donkey, laden with firewood, came up from a side street, almost blocking the cortege, prodded by its owner with a long willow staff. The man pulled hard on the bridle, stopped, then crossed himself in reverence.

Sitting on the circular steps of the stone cross in the middle of the piazza, the old deaf-mute crossed himself also as the cortege passed by. He was the tailor who stitched together the black suit the dead man was wearing. He too worked all night to have the garment ready for next day. Although no one would see his work, he was pleased nevertheless.

By the monument to the Fallen Soldier, old Caterina, on her way to fetch water from the fountain, stopped briefly to allow the funeral procession to go by. An old saying in the village goes like this: "Never come across the path of someone going to his eternal resting-place. It will slow down his entrance into Purgatory."

"This funeral was the poorest of poor funerals," my uncle told me later. "But, at least, no one can say that not even a dog attended." He laughed sardonically. Remo well knew that there would be no money for him at the end of the day. Nor would the priest expect a fee in kind for his services; there was no grain in the old man's granary to give and none of the town's folks had contributed in kind. And, the pallbearers? Well, one day it would be their turn to be carried away to the cemetery by some other good souls of the village. The villagers understood this ancient code of behaviour. You attend someone's funeral in the expectation that one day it will be others assisting in yours. These four men and the three old women were, perhaps, the last on a list, unwritten, of good deeds required of one on earth. It was their turn to serve. It is certain that the old man did his part in his lifetime. The end comes for all. No one deserves humiliation and ignominy in death.

The pace picked up along Via Delle Aie, finally arriving at the cemetery, located away from town near the threshing grounds used at harvest time. The route to the burial place passed by a terraced slope flanked by slender, deep-green cypresses. The smell of pines was everywhere and the cicadas' song filled the air. We slowly climbed the steep grade, especially hard for the pallbearers carrying the heavy coffin. Inside the walled enclosure small flocks of sheep and goats were feeding among the headstones. They scattered as soon as the cortege appeared. A girl tending them quickly herded them outside.

The priest performed a final hurried service, blessing the casket with holy water. He removed the sash around his neck and bent down to remove nits on his black cassock, departing soon after. The men placed the coffin on two wooden trestles; Uncle Remo approached it and, with a few quick strokes of the hammer, sealed the casket forever. He unscrewed and removed the brass handles from the sides and handed them to me to carry away in my wicker basket. The men lowered the casket slowly into the open grave with ropes. The lone graveyard digger soon covered it with earth.

As we were leaving the grounds the distant bell fell silent. The pigeons and the swifts reclaimed their nesting places in the airy lofts of the bell tower and another soul ascended to the heights beyond.

## Note

1. First published in Osvaldo Zappa's memoir *Giovanni's Journey* (Montreal: Cusmano, 2010).

# Building My Bridge Home

*Maria Lisella*

I GREW UP IN A HOUSEHOLD of three generations, speaking the southern Italian dialect of Calabrese alongside English; much later I enrolled in a study abroad program to learn Italian. Continuing to learn the language has enriched my sense of place – yet I am haunted when I visit Italy, feel a strong link to places of my ancestors yet do not totally belong and as much as I may have been Anglo-Saxonized in America, I consider myself apart from the American culture.

### "C'era una volta" or Once Upon a Time

Snow White appeared with Seven Dwarves
a first impression of men and women
that led to questions:
Could it be that women get
seven little men to serve them? Or,
did they stand for seven deadly sins?
Cinderella or *Cenerentola*, the abused bastard
of a houseful of spiteful hens came
close behind, followed
by Little Red Riding Hood, Rapunzel,
unimaginative blondes who tossed
their hair out windows or wore
braids wrapped like little crowns.

I knew them for what they were
"paper dollies," no one would want
to be like for more than a minute
because they'd blow away.

Instead, I waited to sit silently
among *i vecchietti* on Saturday mornings
to watch *Continental Miniatures'*
black and white edgy heroines
like the wild-eyed Anna Magnani,
sweaty, bloody, hair as black as crows
and opera as common as the tar on streets.

Unlike American parents,
Italian *nonni* never sheltered me
from impassioned tales of fallen women.
Magnani's Mamma Roma's midriff rolled
through cheap black satin cloth,
as she fended off old tricks on her journey
to right her life, sell fresh fruit,
win her son back, she flies
into the snare of madness,
in a dialect I always understood.

My love of "things foreign" began, but did not end, in a working class, predominantly African-American neighborhood in Jamaica, Queens, New York. I was the first among my family members to return to Italy nearly 40 years ago, thereby sparking new relationships with second and third cousins, none of whom have visited America. As much as I wish to claim my heritage, my impulse is laced with fear and a sense that I am an impostor – not being all American or all Italian.

### Cornrows[1]

Cheryl's cornrows are
A maze of braids that crisscross
her round head that tops
her dark, Trinidadian neck.

Her mother jelly-coats
her coffee-colored fingers to move
rapid and sure through nappy, crinkled hair.

She pulls one rope of hair
over the other, over the other,
over the other, until
the braids are locked down tight
with barrettes, ribbons and bows.

Around the corner at Jean's Beauty Parlor

white women plop into wide leather chairs
as metallic chemicals crimp and whip
their soft hair into prim tootsie roll curls.

Across the street Sylvia's is crammed
arm to shiny bronze arm with black women
pressing their hair – make it straight, straight,
straight, shiny, smooth as seals – take the nap out.

Cheryl and I watch Angela Davis,
who never lived in Queens,
the land of smooth and straight,
cry out of the TV.

She raises her fist past a brazen halo
of naturally kinky hair –
letting her 'fro fly loud and free,
as if her hair said, "I will not hide,
I am trouble, see me now."

Cheryl's cornrows, a puzzle of braids
locked down tight, tight, tight.
I touch my smooth hair,
a single rope down my spine
wishing all the while
best friends could look more alike.

Of all the places I have visited the world over, in my profession as a travel writer, my fondness for Italy continues to grow. Through my work, I have had opportunities to visit most of the country; however, these trips have taken me not to the places of my ancestors but to other corners of Italy for which I have nothing but curiosity and now some insight.

Continuing to practice and learn the language has given me a deeper sense of place and belonging, but always returning to the U.S. I identify myself as a bridge both in my private life in my family among the generations in Italy and the immigrants in my cultural identity.

My Italian cousins have asked me the same questions over and over – "Aren't you sorry your grandparents left Italy"? and "Why are you so fond of Italy"? – both of which spurred me to address this chasm of misunderstanding in poetry and in journal writing.

Having the good fortune to live in New York City, I am fed by the flow of new immigrants from all over the world, which stoke the fires of my own multi-cultural identity with empathy for the next immigrant.

### The Same[2]

I want to tell
the little Chinese women
with the loud voices
to sit beside each other
so they don't shout
across the car,
over my head,
shattering my space,
interrupting my reading.
I offer my seat.
The lady with the
short-cropped perm
red as a rooster's comb
in a Chinese market
gives me a toothy grin
an essence of onions, garlic
shakes her head
from side to side like a
tai chi exercise, no, no, no
as if to say, "I may shop in Costco
wear jeans, a North Face down jacket
but you'll never
make me a Westerner,
won't drop
my Chinese voice
a single decibel
to suit you and your
Anglo-silence on subway cars
as if they were chapels or
worse, private property."
I hear my grandmother's
staccato Calabrese vowels
clang against brick walls
in an alleyway in Queens
with the same defiance,
the same pride
the same sorrow to be in America.

## Notes

1. First published in LIPS, 2009.

2. First published in *The Paterson Literary Review*, 2007. Editor's Choice for Allen Ginsburg Poetry Award 2006.

# Two Poems

### *Caroline Morgan Di Giovanni*

## A Mountain Like a Ship
*At Roccacaramanico, Abruzzo*

The air is clear above us
we float in the surrounding sky
beneath us solid rock
unmoved for millennia
the ageless grass feeds
millennial sheep, watched over by
generations of shepherds.

Like the wind above the sea
nothing else exists for us
sun burning down
cloud formations gathering, drifting,
the foreknowledge of rain.

Sailors and mountain dwellers
disdain city clutter
crash and noise of the urban landscape
where sun wind and sky go unnoticed,
a choking sensation
unnerves us.

On this summit water earth and air
form the brilliant combination
eagles and hawks soar high
over mountain passes
just as seagulls navigate
the far-off azure oceans.

We are spectators in this place
crouched as in a child's game
glimpse of the privileged location
Madre Terra, Mother of Mountains.

## Umbria

The window opens to a patch of green
geometric olive trees
rustle in the wind
branches aghast
in rolls the fog
green melds to grey,
obscuring all
there where the hill ascends.

The grape vines quiver
meticulous cultivation
welcomes rain
sweet beneficial water washes down
lightening illuminates the scene.

My eye takes in this savage beauty
like a chalice receiving wine
a moment only
in the course of nature
my nature and my life
pause for reflection.

# My Husband Lives in My Garage[1]

## Linda Morra

WHEN I FIRST TOLD OTHERS that my husband, Andrej, was living in my garage, they thought I spoke metaphorically – that he was "in my bad books," as they say, or that he was "in the doghouse" for bad behaviour. We really weren't on bad terms at all; our separation had been peaceably carried out.

So when I shook my head and said, "No, really, he *lives* there," most people looked somewhat puzzled, then disturbed. I suppose that was a natural response. Only my father was visibly pleased, predictably, and in a way that only my father could be.

"So," he nodded self-righteously. "That's what the bum deserves – *disgraziato*. To live in a woman's garage!" He had his reasons for such contempt, even if I disagreed with him.

I had met Andrej over ten years ago, at my father's store, *Ernesto's Hardware*. Not a very imaginative name, yet everyone in the Italian community came to know and to trust my father through his business. His name and reputation were what counted. My father boasted he was a self-made man; he had come over from Italy and set up shop and made his own business successful. He was rightly proud about that.

As a child, I was fascinated by the store: the various metal parts, tools, brushes, paints, and other knick-knacks that stocked the shelves. As his only daughter, I was not permitted to work there. Instead, I would go in and play with these items and listen to my father, who whistled with complex trills, more beautifully than anyone else I had ever heard, then and since. Sometimes, I would sit on a stool behind the counter and watch him, a stocky and strong man, as he worked and whistled. I wondered how my father could make sense of the odds and ends he sold there. I could never decipher much about their purpose beyond the beauty of sound I would elicit when I played with them. Some of his customers didn't know their purpose either. I would try to pay close attention when my father would unpack the secrets of these parts, yet I never understood well. He was a magician, conjuring up results from the most mysterious bits of metal.

While his thick, wavy curls were still a striking blue-black, my father had taken Andrej in as an assistant. He had initially – and unusually – hired him to do some menial tasks in his hardware store. I say "unusual" because it was more typical to have hired one of the sons of his Italian friends. For reasons that even my father never divulged, he liked him enough or felt sorry enough to give him a job. Without a son, my father needed someone who might eventually look after the store. At least, that was the logic I applied when I became involved with Andrej.

It wasn't long after he was hired that he began to pay special attention to me. He had a beautiful, resonant voice, unlike any other I had ever heard. He was extremely polite with those who came into the store, so he was eventually permitted to move beyond tidying the store to waiting on customers. He explained patiently how to use glues, what kind of nails to buy, how to make repairs to virtually anything asked of him. When language failed, as it often did because he spoke little to no Italian, he gestured elaborately. My father seemed to like him immensely.

It is possible that Andrej had hopes of working his way up into my father's books. Instead, he made his way into my bed. That would work just as well, I had thought.

It didn't. My father never quite forgave him for it.

We didn't tell my father about our plans right away. But, when he discovered Andrej and I were getting married, he was outraged almost to the point of not speaking to me. It was bad enough he wasn't Italian, he fumed, but he wasn't Catholic either. His auburn hair and awkwardly tall frame gave away his non-Italian status: Andrej was, in fact, Polish. He was also agnostic. My father couldn't forgive him for such transgressions – not being Italian, not being Catholic. He said he would *never* become used to the idea. Even when I was engaged and still lived with my father, he would mutter to me about it at night.

"*Lui non è buono*, Miranda." He grumbled over his accounting books, which he subsequently withheld from Andrej. If Andrej had

had ideas about taking over my father's business, they stopped when he took up with me.

My father firmly believed marriage was forever. Certain things were sacred – including his favourite pasta dish, the one I still tried to make as my mother had so frequently done before she died when I was only twelve. So, when Andrej and I were separated three years after our marriage, my father was humiliated. He brooded and went around playing the part of the injured hero from some lesser-known opera. His imported sense of Italian pride and Catholic decency, and his immaculate reputation had been hurt. But he also felt vindicated and gloated.

"I told you he was no good." He shook his by then greying curls knowingly. "You should have married a Catholic."

To make our separation official, I moved back home with my father. That's when he began bringing from work stories he had heard about other Italians in Woodbridge who had sons and daughters going through divorces.

"Hey, remember the girl – what's her name – Lucia, just down the street? They have two kids – remember her? Her husband left her and the kids. Just like that," he said, snapping his fingers.

"Lucky I didn't have kids, I guess."

"To be a grandfather," he replied wistfully. *"Non sono così fortunato."* It was hard to win any argument against my father.

On another occasion he asked, "Do you remember that nice couple we met at your uncle Silvio's wedding? The ones sitting at our table?"

"You mean the ones who kept bragging about their condo in Florida and her 2.5 karat engagement ring?"

"And what did Andrej buy you?"

I wouldn't answer that one. Andrej was dirt poor when we married. Working at the store wasn't the most lucrative position. He couldn't afford the appropriate bargaining chip – a very expensive ring – among other things. My father unswervingly believed that only a non-Catholic non-Italian would be so cheap with his daughter.

"Anyway, that couple is getting a divorce too. He found her with another man. And the other man was his *best friend!*"

"I guess a large diamond is no guarantee of a good marriage." I couldn't resist the opportunity of gaining an advantage.

"And I guess a small one is no guarantee either," he retorted, his dark eyes squinting their meaning at me.

I asked him if he wanted an espresso *ristretto* and said no more. It was always like that – he found comfort in knowing that the children of his Italian friends and other members of our community had also suffered disastrous marriages. But he wouldn't let me forget mine either. It was just his way.

It was hard, then, to explain why I allowed Andrej to stay in the garage of the semi-detached house I bought later – with some help from my father, of course, who had withheld that financial help from us when we were married, as a register of his disapproval. Andrej and I had lived in an apartment in downtown Toronto. After our separation, he lived in an even smaller one by himself. He had been struggling with his business and so he began to use my garage as a secondary workplace. He bought mysterious equipment to make some kind of tool – I never understood exactly what it was – and he was unable to accommodate that equipment in the small apartment in which he then lived.

I never quite understood his work. It was a different language to me – guttural, unsophisticated, even barbaric. He swore it had a music of its own, if I only listened closely enough. Since I eventually became a high school teacher of music, I loved the art and all its wonders. But he was as seemingly uninterested in my work as I was in his. It naturally followed that, after three years of marriage, we had little to say to each other. Most of the communication, I suppose, had been physical.

Still he tried to explain to me the nature of this new machinery, this new business. He said he needed the space in my garage to set up the equipment. I could have said no, but there didn't seem to be any reason not to let him. I also felt I owed him something, although I had considered that we were both responsible for our marriage falling apart. After a while, as it began to get warm in the spring and the winter's fierceness ebbed away, he began to move smaller things in – a small suitcase of clothes, some toiletries, a radio. I voiced protest about these small invasions, although not enough to stop him from proceeding.

By July, I began to find some small comfort in his being there regularly. I liked that he was there when I needed help with odd jobs around the house. I reasoned that, aside from using the space in the garage, he really would only come in to use the bathroom on occasion. Besides, when he worked on his machinery, I began to enjoy sitting on the bottom step of a small ladder. I was mesmerized by the rhythm of his movements, his long arms making beautiful strokes. He would often work late into the evenings, so I took up making supper and bringing it out to him as he worked, and then, later, sipping iced coffee and watching while he smiled and squinted at me through the dust thrown up in the garage. I loved hearing the quiet hushed sound as he wiped down the shelves upon which he was seemingly organizing the chaos of things he had brought with him.

We still didn't talk much. One evening, though, I told him my father didn't approve of his being there. He smiled grimly and said, "You've never been so different from your father, Miranda."

I was stunned. "What the hell is that supposed to mean? I am letting you work in *my* garage, Andrej!"

He merely shrugged. I registered my hostility by brusquely leaving him to his work and refrained from visiting him for about a week.

But then came the day when I arrived home to find that Andrej had set up a cot in the corner of the garage.

"The 'No Means No' campaign is clearly taking effect here," I said, mildly irritated.

He smiled without saying anything – he had always been a man of few words. He turned away to straighten up a red blanket over the cot and raise the volume of the radio.

And so my visits to the garage continued.

It didn't occur to me that his presence there might cause problems until about the third week of August, when I brought out some iced coffee for him.

"I have a date tonight," I said. I did and I felt, understandably, somewhat anxious. I had been seeing this man long enough so that I expected him to stay over and I didn't want to explain to him that my husband had taken up living in my garage. I waited a few moments. Andrej didn't turn around, so I left him to work on his machinery.

When my date arrived later that evening, I found myself explaining: "My husband is living in my garage." My date looked as if either he needed a strong drink or I needed one. He glanced at the front entrance, as if he were trying to figure out how to back away through the doorway slowly. *No sudden moves*, I thought I heard him thinking.

"No, no – it's okay," I assured him. "We're not…" I hesitated. I couldn't say we were divorced. We had never filed for one. Although we also didn't live together, it was almost true that we did. And I refused to admit we weren't sleeping together, although we weren't, because, thinking of my bed, I realized I didn't want to put that thought in my date's mind and shut out any possibility of heading in just that direction later on.

"We've been separated for some time. This is just a convenient temporary arrangement," I finally said. My date nodded sympathetically.

If he didn't really understand, he didn't let on. One of those nice Italian boys, the kind of whom my father would have approved, he sat at the table and was complimentary about all I had prepared. For reasons that defied me, I felt thoroughly bored.

He wasn't so nice that I couldn't take him to bed later. I hoped that he'd be better there than at the supper table.

He was.

Yet I couldn't stop thinking about the cot in the garage. With all the windows wide open in the summer heat, I found myself initially curbing my expressions of sexual pleasure for fear I had an audience of one not far out of earshot. Then, oddly, perhaps because I was thinking of that audience of one, I begin to perform really well – long, healthy moans that would have made a porn star blush.

I never heard from my date again.

My career as a porn-star had been short-lived.

"Dammit, Andrej!" I found myself shrieking at him a few days later upon returning home and finding him painting some equipment in the garage. "Why are you *still* here?" I yelled and kicked viciously at an open can of paint. It didn't tip, but slammed into the table between us. Paint splashed up in the air. In the most admirable cascade, it fell – everywhere. Andrej even had globs of paint on his face. Looking down, I saw droplets all over my black silk skirt.

My outburst was followed only by the steady hum of a light-bulb dangling from the ceiling. Then, Andrej picked up a rag to wipe some of the paint slowly from his face.

At length, he spoke across the silence that had lodged itself between us. "I don't know," he finally said musingly. He studied me quietly for a moment. "Maybe I don't want to leave." He smiled ever so slightly but, in part because of the paint that had splashed up on the lenses of his glasses and in part because of the light refracting from the ceiling bulb, I could see neither his eyes nor the intention that might have been expressed there.

He went back to cleaning up the spilt paint.

"I'm making iced coffee," I finally remarked. "Can I bring you some?"

He was carefully studying the can of paint he was re-sealing as he slowly said, "When I'm done here, I'll come in."

## Note

1. First published in *Accenti Magazine,* Issue 22 (Summer 2011), 20-22. This story received Honourable Mention in the fifth annual *Accenti Magazine* writing contest.

# Growth

*Mike Dell'Aquila*

MY GRANDPARENTS ONLY EVER MADE one trip to our home in upstate New York. We relocated after my father took a job at a privately funded geological research institute and were still getting used to the strange dimensions of a rural American town. As far as I knew, neither of my grandparents ever traveled outside of a small radius surrounding familiar quarters in the old neighborhood. Grandpa Sforza had been naturalized, but his American citizenship was nothing more than a piece of paper that allowed him to maintain a hermetic existence more or less undisturbed.

Given my grandfather's anti-American sentiment, it was a bit strange to invite him to our new house for Independence Day. My parents were persuasive though, and after using the growing children as leverage, they were able to successfully talk them into making the drive upstate.

Grandpa Sforza's car was hardly road worthy. It hadn't left their garage in years and the small rust spots that formed around the undercarriage had spread to the doors and side panels of his old sedan. My grandfather commandeered the old boat of a car from the front seat, leaning as far over the wheel as possible. His near-sightedness had worsened to the point of near-blindness, but he had still refused my father's offer to chauffeur them back and forth.

Jumping up at the sound of a busted muffler crawling down the street, I ran to the bay window in the living room and watched their car crawl up our narrow driveway. Behind the broad windshield Grandpa Sforza craned his neck forward and squinted, trying to make sure he found the right place. Our home was just like all the others – we hadn't done anything extreme to stand out in our uniform neighborhood.

"They're here," I called to my parents, who were keeping themselves busy with a laundry list of chores.

"They're here? Already?"

My mother's voice was on edge, stressed because this was her first chance to welcome guests into our new home.

"I'll take care of it," my father responded, hustling down the hallway and heading out the front door.

I followed him outside and stood on the front porch in bare feet. The sun hadn't risen over the hills, so the air was cool enough to tolerate, though still very thick.

Grandpa Sforza got out of the car and stretched. He was overdressed, as usual, wearing a button-down shirt, a sweater vest and pleated trousers. A fedora covered his bald head, completing his dressed-up look. Despite having all of his vestments custom-tailored, he'd lost a significant amount of weight and his clothes hung on him like the drooping branches of a weeping willow.

"*Lorenzo, come stai*," Grandpa Sforza said to my father. He continued a series of questions in Italian.

Grandma Sforza slowly got out of the passenger side and smiled in my direction. "Look at how much you've grown," she exclaimed.

I nodded and answered, "I'm taller than my father now."

It was true, though not by much, and only noticeable if I stood on my tiptoes in pictures.

"*Don Antonio*," Grandpa Sforza called. "*Vieni qua!*"

As always, I did what I was told and ran over to him. He put his hands on my shoulders, kissed both cheeks and then gave me a trademark slap with his right hand. After a quick appraisal, he took off his fedora and placed it on my head.

"You're a real Sforza," my grandfather informed me by way of my father.

"Let's go see the house," Grandma Sforza interrupted. "It's too humid out here. You know that's what does it, right Lorenzo? It's the humidity that makes it unbearable, not the heat."

"You're right, it is the humidity," my father said, grabbing her overnight bag from the back seat. "And today's index is pretty high."

Grandpa Sforza carried his own bag, despite my attempt to become his squire. I watched his gold timepiece twisting around his skinny wrist and listened to the click-clacking of his wingtip oxfords while he walked across our blacktop driveway.

"I just love these colonial homes," Grandma Sforza said, taking the stairs slowly and heavily relying on the banister. "They're so classic and old-fashioned. You'd think a house like this could have been lived in by George Washington himself."

"Mom, this house was built in the early sixties," my father explained. "It's been a part of this country for about as long as we have."

I watched all of this from the bottom step. Grandpa Sforza looked at the home's exterior when he was close enough for it to come into view. Nothing impressed him. He just shrugged his shoulders and kept walking. I adjusted the fedora on my head, pulling it down a bit like a gangster in some film noir movie.

"The house is so beautiful, Anna," Grandma Sforza exclaimed to my mother as the adults made their way inside.

I waited for the front door to close so I could catch my reflection in the glass. The man I hoped to find was instead an awkward, lanky teenager. It was the same reflection I always saw, only with a tan fedora placed on top of my bowl-cut hair.

Inside, the family gathered in our living room. Grandpa Sforza sat in the armchair in the corner, away from the rest of us. My grandmother took the rocking chair, just like she would have in her own home. My mother and my brother Vince sat at opposite ends of the sofa against the back wall. I stood next to my father, assuming the same position with my arms folded across my chest.

"This town is so perfect," Grandma Sforza said, toying with the buckles and metallic embellishments on the purse in her lap. "The drive up was so scenic, too. It's exactly what I used to dream of when I was a little girl. This is the real America, not some cramped apartment by the docks."

"It's such a great place to raise a family, isn't it?" my mother asked. "And it's not too far from Larry's new office."

"Oh, it's all so wonderful," Grandma Sforza said again.

"Just wait until you see the lake," my mother added, already beaming from the compliments. "That's where we're going to see the fireworks."

"And how do you boys like your new home?" Grandma Sforza asked both of us.

"It's great," Vince answered quickly.

I didn't share his feelings on the issue. Since we first moved in, I'd been teased for my accent by the other kids on our block, so I had to practice speaking in a way that would not elicit their laughter. I also tried to stop dressing like a *guido*, as my friends called it. To those ends, I'd been marginally successful, but none of it felt right. Instead of mentioning any of those issues, I just said, "It's different."

"Let me take you on the grand tour," my mother said, rising from the sofa.

Everyone agreed and followed her down the hall. Everyone, that is, except my grandfather and me. I felt like we were conspirators and was happy to stand near his chair as he fished through his bag. Grandpa Sforza moved his clothes around and then removed an unopened bottle of scotch. He held it out and said something, but I wasn't sure what he wanted me to do with it.

"*Cucina*," he said, paring down his language and pointing to the kitchen.

I took the bottle from him and walked up to the counter near the sink. Besides the jugs of Carlo Rossi wine that we kept near the door in the back porch, my parents maintained a dry house. There was no liquor cabinet nor any designated spot in the house for hard alcohol, so I placed his scotch on the counter and left it there, knowing that my grandfather would retrieve it soon enough.

He had other plans, though. I watched him walk through the dining room and then out onto the porch that led to our big wooden deck. He walked right up to the edge, and stared into the thick green forest behind our house.

The tour that my mother was conducting came back through the hallway and then headed downstairs into the basement. No one inquired about my grandfather or me, so I decided to join him outside.

"*Don Antonio*," he said when he saw me. He smiled and said nothing more, knowing that I probably wouldn't understand him anyway.

"I wish I knew how to speak Italian," I said, hoping he might understand. My father always insisted that Grandpa Sforza understood English but simply refused to speak it. I didn't know if there was any truth to that, only that I never once heard him utter a word of the Anglo-Saxon language.

Grandpa Sforza didn't respond right away. He just smoked his cigarette and looked at the dense plant life at the edge of the yard.

"*Vuoi?*" he asked me, holding out the skinny white cigarette.

I didn't have a cool uncle or an older brother who could sneak me sips of beer, a pack of smokes or anything like that, so I jumped at the chance to do something grown-up and rebellious for once. Of course, I did it all wrong. I breathed in as much as I could and I tried to swallow it down like a drink. All I could feel was the presence of smoke in the back of my throat and my eyes watered right before coughing up a big black cloud.

"Bravo," he laughed, taking back the cigarette and tussling my hair with his free hand.

I laughed and coughed and wiped at my eyes.

Pointing to the trees and the hills in the distance, he asked me, "Cue l'America, sì?"

"Sì," I answered, not sure what I was agreeing to and not caring either.

"È brutta," he responded dismissively.

"Sì," I said again, trying to sound more convincing, and then coughing a bit more.

Fourth of July is nothing without fireworks. Any good American knows that. There are other national holidays and other reasons to barbecue with family and friends, but only one day of the year warrants the sky to be lit up and painted with the colors of Old Glory. Our new town was no different: we had an expensive fireworks spectacle that was supposedly choreographed to music, but year after year, it looked like the same shapes appearing in the same order with only a fresh play-list from the local Classic Rock radio station.

We walked down to the lake as a family, moving slowly on my grandmother's account. The sun had started to set an hour before, but the big ball of gas had barely tucked itself behind the mountain on the other side of the lake, so the sky was still lit up and colorful.

"This is just too beautiful," Grandma Sforza exclaimed. "I wish I had my camera. Look at this lake and the trees and the mountains and all the colors in the sky. I wish I could remember this image forever. Isn't it beautiful?"

"It is," my father answered.

"Hey dad," I started to say, hanging back from the family. "Tell grandma and grandpa how this was all formed."

"I don't want to bore anyone," he answered.

"Yes, tell us," my grandmother pleaded. "I don't know anything about natural science. You're the expert, Lorenzo."

"What do you want to know about? The mountain or the lake?"

"Both."

"The mountains are easy to explain," he began. "Basically, the Earth's crust is made up of a series of plates that are in constant friction with one another. Over time, their series of little collisions keeps pushing up layers of rock and soil until we get these gigantic mountains."

"È brutta," Grandpa Sforza said, speaking up for the first time.

"Don't listen to him," my grandmother warned. "He's just being difficult."

"Brutta," Grandpa Sforza said again, nodding as he looked at the mountain in the distance.

"Lorenzo, your father simply cannot appreciate the majesty of the natural world," my grandmother said and then turned to face Grandpa Sforza. "You can't, can you?"

My grandfather raised his index finger and pointed toward the sky. "*Mi fido nel cielo e le stelle.*"

"I trust in the sky and the stars," my father translated.

I looked up. Only the brightest stars were visible, but after night fell in earnest we'd be able to see them all.

Grandpa Sforza waxed poetic about the stars. They were beautiful and only visible at night. Clouds could obscure them, so we were lucky when a clear sky presented itself. They spoke to us, too, and told us the future. The Romans appointed augurs to interpret their movements, and those augurs were the ones who accurately predicted the fates of Romulus and Remus.

"Enough with the sooth-saying," Grandma Sforza said, adding, "*Basta.*"

Moving his balled-up fist up and down, Grandpa Sforza asked, "*Perché?*"

"Because it wasn't an augur that found your tumor. It was a doctor in a lab with X-Ray machines and blood tests. The stars didn't tell you anything."

I looked at my father and then back at my grandfather. Both men had blank expressions.

"*È il mio tempo,*" Grandpa Sforza told us all. It didn't need translation; the finality of his voice was all the confirmation we required.

And with those words, the world stopped spinning for a moment. The powerful inertia slammed me in the chest, robbing me of breath. I did not cry, though. I'd cry later, in the privacy of my bedroom where my tears could turn a pillow dark and damp. At that moment, I fought against childish impulses and remained stoic, just like the two men I stood next to.

"That's all he's been saying since he found out," Grandma Sforza informed us. "And he's been more intolerable than ever."

Over the lake, the first rising balls of light shot up into the sky and their reflections sank to equal and opposite depths. Cheers rung out from the crowd, but my family remained silent. There were, for the next few minutes, a steady cycle of booms and exploding fireworks swiftly sinking down through the thick air toward the water's inconstant surface.

I took a step back and stood beside my grandfather. The scene in the sky was fuzzy, the smoke and thick summer air created a translucent canopy that stretched over our valley. Grandpa Sforza put his hand on my shoulder, gave it a tough squeeze and then left it there. Before the grand finale, there was a pause to let the smoke settle. There was no wind to speak of, but with enough time the haze would dissipate and leave us with a clear black sky.

# Homecoming[1]

### Domenic Cusmano

EXACTLY WHEN MONTREAL'S LITTLE ITALY stopped being a working class neighbourhood and started becoming a trendy nightlife district is uncertain. The process happened gradually, as first- and second-generation Italians left the area for more spacious quarters in the suburbs, and as gritty grocery stores, discount clothing shops and factories gave way to trendy bars and restaurants, jewellery shops and designer clothing boutiques.

The exodus from Little Italy spawned the creation of a number of Italian neighbourhoods across the island of Montreal and beyond – RDP, Laval, Ville Émard, LaSalle, Lachine, St. Michel, Montreal North, Ahuntsic and St. Leonard among others – neighbourhoods where people in the street speak a mix of Italian, English and French a great many decibels higher than elsewhere, where one can buy fresh crusty bread every day at the corner bakery, and where a bar is a place for espresso coffee or gelato.

However, it is the quadrilateral bordered by St. Laurent and St. Denis to the west and east respectively and Jean-Talon and St. Zotique to the north and south (spill-over notwithstanding) that retains the designation of "Little Italy." It is here that the espresso and gelato are tastier, the bread crustier, and watching soccer on a flat-screen TV somehow more meaningful. With few Italian residents left, it is the smattering of Italian businesses that remain and the memories that give the neighbourhood its Italian character.

Only a few decades earlier it seems, Italians were moving in. The rush began in the first decade of the twentieth century, when increasing numbers of Italian labourers, intending to stay temporarily, decided to remain permanently. Abandoning the cramped quarters of the downtown tenements around Dorchester (today's René Lévesque Boulevard) and St. Timothé (Montreal's original Italian district), they made their way north to the Mile-End district where they could find housing more appropriate for the families they called over and lots with a backyard to grow a vegetable garden.

By 1905 the Italians living in Mile End were so numerous that Mass was being celebrated in Italian in the French St. Jean de la Croix Church (now a condo complex) on the corner of St. Laurent and St. Zotique. The community soon demanded its own church. Madonna della Difesa Parish was completed in 1919 on Suzanne Street, renamed Dante Street in 1922, in honour of the great Florentine poet. As the influx of Italians continued, community leaders put forward the idea of erecting an edifice where Italians could congregate and organize their community activities. The Casa d'Italia was inaugurated in 1936.

In 1933, by chance or by design, the Marché du Nord, later rechristened the Jean-Talon Market, opened to the public in an area between Jean-Talon and Mozart that also housed a bus terminal. By the 1960s the bus terminal would be abandoned, and the entire area taken over by *la marchetta*. Vestiges of the old terminal remain in the six parallel "islands" in three rows and adjoining lanes that shape the Market – the two furthest east and the parking lot having since been covered and turned into a year-round, indoor market housing a number of specialty food boutiques.

A market was just what the working class residents of Mile End, now Little Italy, needed. Fresh fruits and vegetables could be had for cheap, and live animals – chickens, rabbits, and on feast days kid and lamb – satisfied the need for fresh meat for many who were versed in the traditional practice of animal slaughter. (The sale of live animals continued until the mid-1960s, when it was banned by city authorities out of concern for hygiene).

As the Italian community became increasingly integrated, leaders commissioned a statue in honour of Giovanni Caboto, which was inaugurated in 1935. It still stands on the corner of St. Catherine and Atwater, though the original inscription the Italians intended, "Discoverer of Canada," was blocked by Montreal City Council for fear it would give umbrage to the French explorer Jacques Cartier who had sailed the waters of the St. Lawrence River 39 years after Caboto had made landfall in Newfoundland. The Italian community's early growth and increasing influence within the society at large was violently disrupted at the start of World War II, when Italian dictator Benito Mussolini, siding with Adolf Hitler's Germany, declared war on the Allies.

Beginning on June 10, 1940, hundreds of prominent Italian Montrealers, many Canadian born, were arrested and given the designation of "enemy alien." None was ever charged with any crime, much less of being a spy or an enemy operative for Italy, yet many were interned for years. The so-called "Internment" of Italian Canadians,[2] which ended in 1945, had a devastating effect on individuals, families and the community as a whole. Italian businesses in Little Italy and elsewhere were forced to close, as men, often the sole breadwinners, were shipped to prisoner-of-war camps in the Canadian bush. A sense of profound shame enveloped the community, which some carry, cross-generationally, to this day. For years, discussion of the subject remained taboo.

Despite several attempts at redress, the Canadian government has never formally acknowledged the impact of its actions. A bill sponsored by St. Leonard Member of Parliament Massimo Pacetti, and passed by the House of Commons in April 2010, required the Canadian government to apologize to the Italian Canadian community in Parliament and institute symbolic reparation for its actions. (The bill was subsequently stalled in the Conservative-dominated Senate and abandoned as a result of the 2011 election.)

But in the ashes of the European war's aftermath lay the foundations for the revival of Little Italy in Montreal. A new wave of Italian immigration swelled the ranks of the community from the second half of the 1940s to the mid-1970s. Many new arrivals established themselves in Little Italy, breathing new life in the quadrilateral and the entire island. New businesses sprang up, and a renewed sense of optimism infused the community.

The influx of young families soon taxed the school system, and caused a schizophrenic reaction within the city's host French-speaking community. While most Italian immigrants gravitated towards English language schools (to the chagrin of radical French nationalists who feared that Montreal would soon become a majority English-speaking city), not a small number of new immigrants who wanted to enter the French school system were turned away. In the 1950s and 1960s a confluence of factors resulted in the creation of dozens of English-language schools throughout the north end of the island including Little Italy where not just the majority but nearly the totality of the student population was ethnic Italian.

\*\*\*

We moved into Little Italy in 1966 and out in 1972. In hindsight, it doesn't feel like we were making history. My parents had merely found an affordable apartment that was slightly less cramped than the one we left behind in Montreal East. Our trajectory followed that of many latter-day Italian immigrants, who saw in Little Italy friendly surroundings and familiar customs – a transitory stop on the way up the social ladder.

Our apartment sat atop a bakery cum restaurant on the corner of Jean-Talon and Casgrain, where the pleasing scent of the restaurant menu wafting from the kitchen air vents fused with the stench of rotting garbage – restaurant detritus – piled up against the back stairs below the bedroom I shared with my brother. These contrasting scents were in some ways symbolic of life conditions in the old neighbourhood – the good and the bad intertwined, the line between the two sometimes impossible to discern. This was equally true of some of the characters who inhabited the neighbourhood – their actions often blurring the line between the lawful and the illicit.

But despite the obstacles and risks, we felt safe and confident within the invisible walls we had created, our sheer numbers nourishing our sense of security. With virtually everything we needed within walking distance and with Italian as the language of every day, we had little reason to venture out. Though hardly idyllic, we were self-satisfied in our village within a village.

My first job at the age of eleven was at the Market selling flowers for twenty-five cents an hour after school and on Saturdays. Long before we had any conception of bicycle paths, tennis lessons, and summer art camp, we rode our bicycles within the confines of the Market after the stalls closed and the cars were gone – a safe, concrete park, all to ourselves and the other neighbourhood kids.

When we weren't riding our bikes or getting into the occasional fight, we would play at catching flies – whose density in our area, because of the Market, far exceeded the norm – and keeping them in Mason jars. In winter, we played hockey in a makeshift outdoor rink on one of the Market parking lots – our house serving as the hockey dressing room for my schoolmates and me.

At different times in the summer, a procession in honour of the patron saint of some Italian town would wind its way around the narrow streets, always finding passage through the Market. From our front-row seats on our second-story balcony we observed the men, women and children in costume chanting in unison, led by someone with a bullhorn, and a life-size plaster reproduction of the saint. On Sunday mornings we watched *Teledomenica*, the mother of Italian television programming in Montreal. What the show lacked in finesse, it made up for in charm.

We were jolted into the reality of events outside our invisible walls one morning in October 1970, when we saw soldiers in full battle gear standing guard around the police station down the street and by other vital buildings around the Market. The effect of seeing soldiers patrolling city streets on a twelve-year-old boy is at once exciting and disconcerting. For our parents, with memories of the chaos and carnage of World War II still lingering, the sight of armed soldiers on patrol was rather alarming.

The FLQ-instigated October Crisis had breached our perimeter. Though hardly at the root of the problem, by the mere act of sending their children to English school, Italians were unwittingly exacerbating political tensions. One year earlier, the St. Leonard Riot, though a minor footnote in the city's history, had polarized people along linguistic lines.

Fortunately, a conflict that could have had serious societal repercussions was effectively diffused by the authorities. A succession of language and education laws, culminating in Bill 101 – a law that annoyed some for being too severe and angered others for not being severe enough – settled the issue by making French Quebec's only official language and by restricting but not banning access to English school.

\*\*\*

In the meantime, the Italian community was adapting and growing. Greater numbers among the second generation, who attended university and joined the professional ranks or started businesses, didn't feel the need or the desire to huddle together. The conditions that insulated the inhabitants of Little Italy eventually felt stifling, blocking access to the broader society. Greener pastures lay outside the village walls.

With Little Italy no longer the single focus of Italian Montreal affairs, its role is being redefined as a locus of style and fine living, an emblem of *la dolce vita*. St. Laurent Boulevard is where Formula

1 racing aficionados gather in June to admire Ferraris in anticipation of the Canadian Grand Prix and where in August the city celebrates "Italian Week." Massive crowds spontaneously swarmed into the old district in 1982 and 2006 when the Italian soccer team won the World Cup – a subconscious desire to return to the womb, psychologists might argue. The symbols and appeal of Italianness in the neighbourhood are evident, but much has changed.

This evolution in some ways mirrors the transformation of Italian Montrealers themselves, from an inward looking and cautious people composed mostly of labourers to a sometimes brash and overconfident horde of business people and professionals who bridge the city's English-French divide.

What was once seen as a ghetto, inhabited by an exotic people with strange eating and social habits, is now a vibrant part of the city, where people gather to celebrate and simply enjoy life. Because of a critical mass that resisted assimilation long enough, the Italians of Little Italy were able to leave their mark. Some of their quirks, like eating outdoors, drinking wine with a meal and having a passion for soccer (not an easy feat in hockey-mad Montreal!) have become mainstream.

For all the comforts of living in the suburbs, it is still in Little Italy that Italian Montrealers like to gather. Today, when I find myself sipping a cappuccino or enjoying a pizza at a sidewalk caffé in Little Italy, even though I know I am just visiting, I feel like I've come home.

## Notes

1. First published in *Accenti Magazine*, Issue 19 (Summer 2010) under the title: "Little Italy, Montreal: Redefining the Old Neighbourhood."

2. See two books published in 2012: *Beyond Barbed Wire: Essays on the Internment of Italian Canadians* and *Behind Barbed Wire: Creative Works on the Internment of Italian Canadians* (eds. Licia Canton, Domenic Cusmano, Michael Mirolla, Jim Zucchero), available at www.guernicaeditions.com/free_ebooks.php.

# Dominique

*Excerpt from a work in progress*

## John Calabro

LYING IN BED IN HIS underwear Pierre is smoking nervously, even though he promised me he wouldn't smoke in our hotel room. I know Pierre from work, although I wouldn't call what he does work. But then I am to blame since two years earlier I had enthusiastically hired him to do French translations for the Ontario Ministry of the Environment, where I report to the Deputy. Pierre is in his mid-thirties, originally from Montreal. He had a good resumé and interviewed well. I later found out that Pierre didn't like deadlines, drank heavily, snorted recreationally, smoked weed, and popped enough pills for me to find him interesting and to consider him somewhat of a friend, and a sometimes imbecile.

I should have fired him a long time ago, but as an act of rebellion against my own bosses, I hadn't. I had other issues. One of which is allowing people to convince me to do things I don't care for, like dragging me to San Francisco. But then I had an idea that I could use this trip to fulfil a promise I had made to myself a while ago.

"So you like my sister."

He gets up and fixes us a drink. There must be at least eight ounces of vodka in the glass. He is pouring alcohol as if it is mineral water. His tone is one of sarcasm. He is angry, and since I haven't done anything wrong, I assume that the result of the football game he had gone to see, while his sister and I went for a walk, was not to his liking.

"She's nice, very pretty. Smart too. She wants to be a writer; I'd love to see her work."

"Yeah, yeah, yeah. I'm sure you'd like to see something else."

He was being a jerk and it could only mean one thing.

"Why are you being an asshole, Pierre? How much did you lose?"

When pressed, he explains that the *fucking* 49ers missed a *fucking* field goal in the dying minutes of the game and it cost him a *fucking* bundle. It had been a sure thing. The *fucking* kicker, Martinez, who had been a perfect ten for ten until that day, and who'd successfully kicked hundreds from further away, missed a *fucking*, easy as pie, 28-yarder.

"*Fuck* him."

He makes a fist and smashes it down on the Colonial dresser, whose hard wood thankfully sustains Pierre's anger without splintering under the force.

"*Fuck!*" He screams in pain.

I ask him if the loss was more than what he had won on the previous day's Jays' game, but he doesn't answer. He gets another drink, having spilled the last one. I guess I'll know soon enough. If the loss is too high, his bookie would be phoning. Pierre shrugs it off, pretends that it's not a big deal and goes back to drinking and to talking about his sister.

"I'll work it out, you know I always do. Did Dominique ask you about me, did she pump you for information?"

He gets up, comes over, and two inches from my face with alcohol fuelled spit and finger tapping on my chest he makes his point.

"Don't say anything. Nothing, not a word, *nada*, nothing about me, you understand. I'll fucking kill you if you do."

"Okay, okay, take it easy. Why didn't you ever tell me about her?"

We had been in San Francisco barely a day when this mysterious sister of his shows up. He introduced me as his Sicilian, Mafia boss; which he thought was funny, and she didn't. After that, I had a hard time convincing her that I truly was Sicilian, not in the Mafia and not even a good boss.

"Nothing to tell. We used to be close, and then we were not. Now she's always on the move, travels all around the country; works for some big shot in Vancouver. Recently she's gotten to calling me. She thinks I'm sick. She thinks I need mothering. She wants to be a good sister. I don't need a mother or a sister; I made the mistake of telling her I was coming to Frisco."

He drains his glass and lights up again. To my protests and stern reminder that he promised not to smoke in the room, he answers that it doesn't count because it's a joint. I won't bother asking where he got it. I watch him as he puffs and fills his glass again. He loves his Grey Goose.

Pierre was right; Dominique had asked several times about him.

*"Does he drink a lot?"* she said.

*"No, not really,"* I said.

I had lied even before he told me to lie. What he did or didn't do was his business. I didn't care to get involved, which is why he liked me. I didn't judge. How could I have said to his sister that I've seen him at clubs do ecstasy, smoke a joint, and chase it down with a bottle of beer, and then ask for a double Grey Goose, neat? And besides, drinking will be the least of his problems if he really lost big on that 49ers game and can't find the cash for his bookie. Pierre seemed to be gambling more and more, and that I didn't understand.

Earlier, while Dominique kept questioning me, all I could think of was how stunning she was. She had that understated, chic European look, with long dark hair cut in a Cleopatra style that framed her bright brown eyes and lips she had shaded with a subtle pink. She reminded me of the actress Juliette Binoche in her earlier films. I didn't want to talk about her brother and so I asked what she liked to do for fun, what excited her. She got very animated and for a moment forgot about him.

*"I write."*

*"Poetry?"*

*"No, fiction."*

She went on to talk about the novel she was working on; it was almost finished. She told me about how she wanted to get it published; and how she was frightened to death of sending it out. For a moment, as she spoke, she seemed so vulnerable and it made her even more beautiful. I could easily fall in love.

*"It's nice to see so much passion. Most people I know go through life with limited interest."*

I was speaking mostly about myself. Dominique smiled, and like an idiot I thought that I was making a connection.

*"Does he have friends? Do you think he's happy?"*

*"I guess so."*

She was persistent. She didn't really want to know about me and maybe Pierre was right. I had found it difficult to be vague, and I think she knew that I wasn't forthcoming with any real answers. I hadn't paid too much attention to her inquiries until Pierre brought it up. I didn't like that he implied that his sister was using me. It did sound suspicious. I mean she asked me to go for a walk, and I am not the kind of guy women ask out. On the other hand she was very beautiful, and so what if I let her use me. In effect I probably would betray Pierre if she pushed a little harder. It wouldn't take much, maybe just a kiss...

"Are you asleep?" Pierre calls out.

I was drifting, thinking of his sister, wondering about what she really wanted, but also wondering what kissing her would be like. I had never kissed such a gorgeous woman before... here I was being an idiot again. We had been silent for a while, the room was dark, the smell of grass was no longer unpleasant, and for a moment I thought of pretending I was asleep and not answer him.

"No."

"I don't just have a sister, I also have a brother, Michel... had a brother I should say; he died."

Now he has my attention. I sit up and wonder why he is saying that.

"I'm sorry. When?"

"Long time ago, almost fifteen years..."

I try not to show any surprise. Dominique had also talked about her brother.

"He was young," I say.

"Yeah, Dominique was fourteen when he passed away."

"How did he die?"

He paused. It could have been for effect; Pierre was never at a loss for words.

"Killed himself."

"Holy shit, you're kidding, how did it happen? You've never said anything."

"It's not something I like to talk about. My father found him. My dad had his own problems; always distant, he had withdrawn even more. He sold life insurance and had a love-hate relationship with it. He blamed his unhappiness on work, on my mother, on his friends, on his co-workers, on us, on society, on everybody, you know what I mean. He hated people, drank himself to sleep most nights, but he loved Michel. Michel was the smart one, the funny one, the sensitive one: he was going places, unlike me who was too happy to just fuck up." He pauses, then asks brusquely: "Are you there?"

"Listening..."

"That morning, I woke up to my father screaming for help, yelling from the garage. I was the first one there since my room was above it. The door in the hall that led to the garage was wide open, and there I saw my father holding up Michel. Michel had a rope around his neck.

My father was screaming for help, for anyone to help. I was eighteen years old, two years older than Michel. My brother had tied a noose to the garage ceiling beam and had jumped off the hood of dad's car. 'Grab his legs and push up,' my father screamed while he climbed on the car and tried to loosen the cord. He couldn't do it, but kept trying. 'Don't let go, Pierre.' He was yelling. I hugged Michel's legs and pushed up. After a while my arms got sore, he was so heavy. 'Don't let him die. Hold him up Pierre…' My father climbed down and went looking for something to cut the rope. My arms were cramping up, I was in so much pain, I had to let go. And when I couldn't hold any longer, I did let go, just for a second. Michel's body dropped like a stone, the rope tightened around his throat and made a snapping sound. I shook my arms and quickly grabbed him again. I remember my father screaming, 'You weak son of a bitch. Push up. You're useless. Hold him up …' Dad tried to loosen the rope, but nothing worked. He climbed down, found the stepladder and propped it under Michel's feet while I held him in place. He jumped back on the hood and finally cut the rope with a hack-saw. We laid Michel on the garage floor and my father tried a fumbling, ineffective CPR. He pressed on his chest, did mouth to mouth, while I watched on the side, not knowing what to do. I called 911, but it was all too late. Michel was dead. I can still see his body laying there and my father on his knees beside him, as if it was yesterday."

"I'm sorry. You can't blame yourself…"

"No, no, I do, it was my fault. I hated Michel for being the favourite son, and I always made sure he knew that."

"There must have been other reasons. You couldn't have known."

Pierre asks me to get him another drink and continues talking but with greater difficulty. He is slurring badly, I can barely understand him.

After a moment of silence, I ask him about Dominique and her reaction.

"My mother, like my father, also blamed me, but Dominique, she never said anything."

"I am sorry" is the only thing I can think of saying, and I keep repeating it since I find the whole story very confusing.

"I'm not saying this so that you feel sorry for me, I'm telling you because you are my friend and I trust you. I'm also warning you; don't get involved with my sister. Don't trust her. Dominique can be quite manipulative. She always gets her way; it's because of her good looks."

"Okay. Understood, don't worry."

Of his own volition, he tells me that he bet $50,000 on the game and that he doesn't have the money to cover it. That he'll have to find it somewhere.

"$50,000? Holy shit!"

"It's a bit of a mess, but don't tell Dominique about it. I told you about Michel because I trust you: Sicilians keep their words, right? Remember don't tell my sister anything, not even about Michel. Nothing about what I told you. Swear."

"I swear."

He promptly falls asleep.

What bothered me the most about his confession was not so much the gambling loss or the suicide of his brother, but the fact that Dominique not two hours earlier had told me that her brother Michel was teaching English as a second language to university students in Thailand…

# Del cacciucco le code

*Alberto Mario DeLogu*

Sul pelo liscio di questa landa
non ci sono ferite di ballasola
né visi muconosi d'orfani
né lai di condannati.

Non ci sono domande irrisposte
né torme d'umani sloggiati
né tafani sulle labbra dei moribondi.
Non ci sono amori funamboli
né secreti sparsi.

In questo gigaborgo
non ci sono vicoli né passanti,
ma rue avenide corsi e bulevardi
ed umani stridenti, correnti,
guidanti, apparcanti carri
già ben armati e loccati.

Qui non c'è l'orgoglio barbaro
di chi bilancia la rasoia,
ma basamenti saloni e gazebi
dietro peristili palladiani
e cortine di bricchi bianchi.

Qui del castro rimane il cardo,
di cespi erbe colori e fiori
restano diritti fili verdolastri,
d'urla clamori e richiami
restano flebili sussurrati sibili.

Qui del difficile rimane il facile,
dei boschi la legna,
del cacciucco le code,
del molto il poco,
del tutto l'uno.

# Il suono delle campane

*Pietro Corsi*

TRASCINANDOSI DIETRO LA VALIGIA A rotelle, il Viaggiatore si incamminò lungo la strada che dalla stazione ferroviaria portava al centro storico. Di quella strada conosceva ogni pietra, e delle mura delle case allineate sulla sinistra, come muraglia a protezione dell'abitato, conosceva ogni fessura.

Il suo sguardo andò a posarsi sull'orto, alla sua destra, tra la strada e la ferrovia. E notò, con tristezza, che quella fonte di vita era ora morta. Un giorno, quell'estensione di terreni ai piedi del paese era stata coperta di verde e di oro, dei colori più vivi e più belli della natura. Aveva rifornito ognuno degli abitanti del paese di frutta e di verdure: aglio e cipolla e spinaci, lattughe e cetrioli con i loro fusti vellutati, sedano e prezzemolo con le sue foglioline frastagliate e lobate, basilico, rosmarino, finocchio dolce dalle guaine carnose e bianche, scarola, cime di rape e frutti di stagione. E fiori, fiori di ogni colore per i vivi, crisantemi per i morti.

In quell'orto veniva coltivato di tutto e tutti vi accorrevano per le necessità giornaliere delle loro cucine e delle loro mense. Le donne ci si recavano di mattina presto, facevano la fila e aspettavano pazientemente, chiacchierando di questo e di quello, dei fatti di casa, spesso dei fatti della casa d'altri. Quando arrivava il loro turno chiedevano cosa c'è, cosa c'è. Gli ortolani erano sempre allegri, rispondevano cosa volete, cosa volete: perché tutto c'era, in quell'orto, bastava solo chiedere. Le donne chiedevano questo e chiedevano quello; i giardinieri annuivano, si allontanavano. Andavano a cogliere questo e quello, li mettevano nel grembiule delle massaie e delle serve dei signori. Riscuotevano il giusto prezzo e mettevano i quattrini nelle loro capienti sacche, oppure segnavano con un mozzicone di matita, su un pezzo di carta, il nome della cliente e l'ammontare dovuto, che veniva riscosso a fine mese o a fine anno, a seconda dei casi e della famiglia debitrice.

Arrivò il giorno in cui la gente del paese cominciò a seguire il richiamo di terre lontane che promettevano il chiarore che precede il sorgere del sole, l'aurora, la vita nuova. I primi ad andar via furono i giornalieri e i braccianti, seguiti dai contadini che non avevano terre da coltivare, poi anche da quelli che avevano terreni in proprio. Senza braccianti e senza contadini a cui rendere i loro servizi, anche gli artigiani presero la coraggiosa decisione di seguire quel richiamo pur non sapendo, esattamente, cos'era. Ma un richiamo era, e bisognava seguirlo. A loro volta furono seguiti da quanti, sconsolati, erano stati ammaliati non dal richiamo, ma dall'idea della salvezza.

In paese, dunque, non c'erano più giornalieri, non c'erano braccianti, non c'erano contadini per i campi e le botteghe degli artigiani erano vuote, chiuse. Mentre un giorno, per le strade, si udivano le carezzevoli note dei violini provenienti dalle botteghe dei barbieri, e il dolce suono delle chitarre che piangevano in quelle dei sarti, e le fisarmoniche dei contadini che allegramente intonavano *La Gazza Ladra* o *Il Carnevale di Venezia*, o qualche improvvisato tango argentino, ora quelle stesse strade erano abbandonate: non si udiva altro che il silenzioso trascorrere dei minuti e delle ore, del giorno senza un domani.

E dove una volta si udivano fabbri e ferrai che forgiavano il ferro per un'inferriata o per le calzature dei cavalli, e le seghe dei falegnami che lavoravano il legno grezzo per costruire i mobili dei braccianti dei contadini e degli artigiani, e calzolai che temperavano la pelle di vacca per le suole delle scarpe e la pelle di capretto per le tomaie con i loro ben calibrati martelli a testa quadra e a testa tonda, ora non si udiva altro che il quieto vociare di qualche vecchia distratta che, senza saperlo, a voce alta faceva, a se stessa, come una pazza, domande che non avrebbero mai trovato una risposta.

L'orto del paese, che era stato l'orto di tutti, non c'era più. Abitato da erbacce e da inutili piante spontanee, da spietati topi di campagna, l'orto era morto. Persino gli alberi da frutta, specie quelli di fichi, avevano perduto la loro forza. Emanava, dai loro rami cadenti, dalle foglie smorte e ritorte, un odore asprigno selvatico che ricordava l'abbandono.

Più su, prima della curva, da un cunicolo aperto che, scendendo dalla montagna, attraversava i campi a monte e passava sotto la strada prima di raggiungere la ferrovia e i campi a valle, una volta scorreva un'acqua limpida e fresca, chiara come acqua di sorgente. Andava a lambire le radici degli ortaggi dando loro forza e vita, inebriandoli di sapori conosciuti, familiari, i sapori di casa. Ora non più. Non c'era più acqua e il cunicolo, secco, era anch'esso infestato da erbacce e da animali.

Mentre il Viaggiatore osservava quell'abbandono, un velo di tristezza andava a coprirgli il cuore che palpitava e si fermava, riprendeva a palpitare più forte, e con tristezza cercava di richiamare alla mente i giorni migliori che il paese aveva vissuto: con il chiassoso *bufù* di fine anno, l'Epifania e la Pasquetta, i fuochi di Sant'Antonio Abate, il proverbiale convivio di San Giuseppe con Giuseppe e Maria, i più anziani del quartiere, e gli apostoli, i più giovani; gli affollati forni a legna ai quali accorrevano le casalinghe per il pane per la pizza per i dolci; e la mietitura e la trebbiatura, e il raccolto dell'uva e delle olive; le strade affollate dopo la messa domenicale, i signori che uscivano per farsi vedere dai loro mezzadri e quelli, i mezzadri, i contadini, vestiti a festa come se stessero per andare a un matrimonio. Ricordi sbiaditi, dileguati in un curioso, quasi morboso desiderio di dimenticanza. Come se, insomma, dimenticando, tutto potesse tornare, infine, come una volta.

Aveva appena cominciato a risalire su per la Terravecchia, da sotto l'antica arcata del Palazzo Ducale, quando fu raggiunto dal familiare suono delle campane. Veniva dalla torre campanaria della chiesa madre, lì a due passi da dove si trovava. Din-don; din-din-don, din-don. Le campane ripetevano quel suono prima lentamente poi più in fretta, sempre più in fretta. Le note si susseguivano con dolorosa cadenza, un lamento.

Il Viaggiatore non tardò a riconoscere il significato di quel lamento. Era nato ed era cresciuto all'ombra di quelle campane. Da bambino il sacrestano lo aveva invitato a suonarle per ognuna delle occasioni del giorno: a messa la domenica e ogni sera della settimana, ad acqua con l'avvicinarsi di un temporale, a ventunora per richiamare i contadini a casa, e a festa quando tutte e quattro scampanavano allegramente per la gioia dei festanti. Le aveva suonate anche a morto in qualche occasione osservando, diligentemente, la giusta sequenza dei din e dei don: non potevano esserci errori, lo ammoniva il sacrestano, prima di affidargli quel compito riservato al sacro rito dei morti.

Sapeva perciò che quei dolorosi din-don che si susseguivano con monotona e dolorosa cadenza venivano da due delle quattro campane: il din, un suono timido ma penetrante come un ago, una lama, veniva dalla campana piccola che dava in direzione della stazione; il don invece, un suono imponente, prepotente quasi, veniva da quella più grande che dava sulla Terravecchia. Venivano suonate in quel modo per avvertire la cittadinanza che c'era un morto in paese. La chiesa madre annunciava che uno dei suoi figli aveva intrapreso l'ultimo viaggio. La chiesa madre aspettava un morto, aspettava il suo morto.

Il Viaggiatore risalì, sulla sinistra, la scalinata che dal portone d'ingresso portava alla sua casa, al primo piano. La scalinata a destra portava invece alla casa di suo nonno che aveva seguito il suono delle campane anni prima, prima ancora che lui lasciasse il paese, prima ancora che lasciasse l'Italia per andare incontro al suo incerto destino di migrante senza viso e senza nome, ombra che seguiva altre ombre, a sua volta seguita da ombre in un mondo di ombre.

Fino a qualche anno fa, in quella casa c'era stata sua madre. Anche lei aveva seguito il suono delle campane. Prima o poi tutti seguivano il lugubre richiamo di quelle campane ed entravano in chiesa, venivano portati in chiesa, la loro chiesa. Da lì, attraversavano il paese dal basso in alto, poi da quell'alto proseguivano a sinistra lungo un tratto della SS 87 fino all'uscita dal paese e si affacciavano sulla porta dei cipressi che adornavano i vialoni del camposanto, l'uscita dal mondo.

Il din-don continuava, monotono, riverberava tra le mura delle stanze vuote. Il Viaggiatore sapeva che quella cantilena poteva durare anche dieci, quindici minuti; e quei dieci, quindici minuti avevano il sapore dell'eterno. Quello che non sapeva, che non poteva sapere ancora, era l'identità del morto. Quando anche gli avessero fatto un nome, pensò, con tristezza, non lo avrebbe riconosciuto. Con rabbia, riconosceva il viso della gente che incontrava per strada, ma non il nome. Non ricordava i nomi dei suoi concittadini. Anonimo nel suo nuovo mondo di migrante, quando tornava in paese si ritrovava, anche lì, in un mondo senza nome.

Il Viaggiatore andò alla finestra che dava sulla Terravecchia, la aprì facendo attenzione di non scuoterla troppo. E si ricordò che aveva bisogno di essere riparata, o rimpiazzata. Si affacciò, per vedere se passava qualcuno a cui chiedere notizie del morto. Non passava nessuno. Le campane avevano smesso di suonare. Di lì a poco il morto sarebbe arrivato in chiesa.

Anche la mamma del Viaggiatore si affacciava sempre a quella finestra per vedere se passava qualcuno. E se qualcuno passava, chiedeva cosa c'era di nuovo. Ora sua madre non c'era più. Anche lei aveva seguito il richiamo dei din e dei don delle campane. Con un senso di colpa nel petto, la colpa sempre presente nel petto di ogni migrante, lui era tornato, l'aveva accompagnata lungo il vialone dei cipressi.

Vide una vecchia che svoltava l'angolo della chiesa, gli parve di riconoscerla. Non ne ricordava il nome però. Aspettò che arrivasse sotto la finestra, certamente lei doveva sapere chi era il morto. Poggiata a un bastone, la vecchia camminava a passo lento. Era vestita di nero, come tutte le donne della sua età, e camminava lentamente avanzando con il bastone che faceva tic sui sanpietrini, poi tac, segnando così, con quel suono, ognuno dei suoi passi lenti, lenti come una notte senza luna, una giornata senza sole. Tic... tac... Era un suono breve e secco, metallico. Rimbombando nel vuoto silenzio della Terravecchia ricordava, chissà perché, l'abbandono. Tic, il bastone faceva. Poi, tac. Al tac la vecchia fermava il passo stanco, riposava, poi di nuovo tic.

"*Chije è, ù mùorte, chije è?*" Il Viaggiatore chiese, quando la donna fu sotto la sua finestra, chi è, chi è il morto.

Il bastone si fermò sul tic e lui restò in attesa del tac, che non ci fu. Con un gesto stanco, raddrizzandosi con le due mani poggiate sul bastone, la donna alzò la testa per vedere chi le parlava, chi le chiedeva informazioni sul morto. Riconobbe il Viaggiatore, un sorriso raggiante le apparve sulle labbra raggrinzite dandole grazia e dignità.

"Ah," disse. "*Sié tu, sié remenute.*"

"Sì," lui rispose, "sono tornato." Poi, visto che la donna lo guardava senza rispondere, nuovamente chiese, "Chi è, chi è il morto?"

"Eh!," quella rispose, scuotendo la testa, "*chiie è ... n'u sacce ... dicene ché è nu 'merrecane*," chi è, non lo so, dicono che è un americano. "Per questo è così tardi. I morti, o al mattino o alle quattro. Mai così tardi, mai alle sei di sera."

"*Però, nu 'merrecane?*" il Viaggiatore le fece eco, sorpreso, perché un americano non muore nel suo paese, nessuno muore nel suo paese a meno che non sia del paese. "*E dé dòve è menùte?*" da dove è venuto.

"Eh!, *dé dòve*," la donna rispose, "*nen'zè sà, nu sacce, mo', po' vedeme é tu facc'assèpé,*" di dove, non si sa, non lo so, poi vediamo e te lo faccio sapere.

"*Scine, scine,*" lui disse, facendo un cenno d'intesa con la testa, sì, sì, "*Po' vedeme, po' vedeme,*" poi vediamo.

"E tu," la donna chiese, prima di rimettersi in cammino col suo bastone, "*quande sié menute, quande te ne vié?*"

Sempre così: quando sei arrivato, quando te ne vai. Quelle parole, quelle due domande, a chi non era familiare con le usanze del paese sembrava volessero nascondere un sospetto. Non era così. Era, più semplicemente, il modo di dare il bentornato a chi veniva da fuori, soprattutto a chi veniva dalle Americhe. Come a dire bentornato, sei venuto per restare? Ma nessuno veniva per restare. Solo il morto, ora, quello sì era venuto per restare.

"*So' ppéne arrevate, mò mò, 'nquishtu mémènt,*" sono arrivato or ora, in questo momento, il Viaggiatore rispose, dopo essersi soffermato a pensare al bentornato.

La donna chiese, di nuovo:

"*È quande te ne vié?*" e quando te ne vai.

Il Viaggiatore sorrise. Si ricordò che non aveva risposto alla seconda domanda della donna.

"*Mò, nù sacce,*" disse, non lo so. "*Une de chishti iuorne,*" non lo so, uno di questi giorni.

"*Chishti iuorne... Chishti iuorne, è come a nu taluorne, 'u décève a bbonaneme de mammète,*" la vecchia rispose, questi giorni, questi giorni, è come una lagna, lo diceva la buonanima di tua madre.

Riabbassò la testa, sollevò il bastone a mezz'aria come in segno d'intesa, o di rimprovero, prima di poggiarlo di nuovo a terra con un tac.

"*Shine, mò, è proprie acqu'shì è, è proprie nu taluorne. Pò ce vedeme, eh?*" sì, certo, è proprio così, è proprio una lagna. Poi ci vediamo, sì?, il Viaggiatore rispose.

"*Shine, shine, pò ce vedeme, pò ce vedeme,*" la donna disse, sì, sì, poi ci vediamo.

Riprese il suo cammino. Tic, fece il bastone, al primo passo, poi tac, al secondo passo. Mentre la donna si allontanava, il Viaggiatore non poté fare a meno di notare che il tic accompagnava la gamba destra, il tac quella sinistra. Curva, la donna vestiva di nero come tutte le donne della sua età, come tutte le vecchie e le non più giovani del paese.

Era vestito di nero anche il morto?

Il Viaggiatore richiuse la finestra accompagnandola con le due mani, una in alto, una in basso, per assicurarsi che non ci fosse frizione. Si ricordò del tarlo. Gliene aveva parlato sua madre, lamentandosi del fatto che prima aveva preso dimora in un legno del cesso, la cornice di un vecchio specchio rotto, poi era andato ad abitare in tutti i legni di casa. Quel tarlo aveva logorato anche la finestra, che si era contorta e non chiudeva bene. Doveva farla riparare, o doveva rimpiazzarla con una di quelle moderne, termiche le chiamavano, con intelaiatura in alluminio e doppio vetro. Andò nella camera da letto, aprì la valigia, ne estrasse il rasoio e il pettine, il dentifricio, la saponetta. Si tolse la giacca e la camicia, entrò nel bagno. Si sciacquò il viso, si pettinò guardandosi nello specchio rotto con la cornice abitata dal tarlo.

"Uno di questi giorni," pensò, osservando i bucherellini lasciati dal tarlo, come cacche di mosca, "uno di questi giorni ne compro uno nuovo."

Sempre lo diceva, come sua madre. E sempre, come sua madre, se ne dimenticava. Pensò, intanto, di andare in chiesa. Per vedere il morto. Per sapere da dove veniva il morto.

# La giacca[1]

*Delia De Santis*

(*Traduzione di Gabriella Iacobucci, con una premessa della traduttrice*)

W*RITING OUR WAY HOME*, LETTERALMENTE "scrivere il nostro ritorno." Ma il titolo della Conferenza di Atri è sapientemente vago, suggerisce le più svariate interpretazioni, fa volare la fantasia. Sarà per questo che mi viene in mente un romantico "scrivere per tornare." Ma poi vado oltre, e allontanandomi dal significato originale delle parole mi sposto dal terreno della scrittura a quello della traduzione, un terreno che mi è congeniale. Allora ecco "tornare attraverso la lingua che parlavamo a casa," o "tornare a casa attraverso la lingua che parlavamo"…

L'italiano è la lingua che Delia parlava da ragazzina, prima di partire per il Canada. Ora non lo usa più, ma non lo ha dimenticato. Questa traduzione è il mio piccolo contributo al significato ideale della Conferenza e al legame che mi unisce agli amici scrittori italo canadesi. Infine, è un omaggio a Delia e alla lingua della sua infanzia.

***

"Quanto?" chiede lui, tastando con le dita la pelle, la spalla, il polsino.

"È nuova. Nuova di zecca," dice lei.

"Va bene, ma quanto costa? Avrà un prezzo, no?"

" Ma perché ti arrabbi? E poi perché sei venuto così presto? La vendita comincia alle otto. Non sono ancora pronta."

"Quanto costa? Quanto cazzo costa?"

"Qua sono a casa mia. Tu non hai il diritto di parlare in questo modo a casa mia."

"Diritto, che ne sai tu di diritti. Chiedi a mia madre, lei ne sa qualcosa."

"Non so di che vai parlando," borbotta lei. "Se vuoi quella maledetta giacca, ecco, prendi. Apparteneva a una persona speciale. Non voglio più tenerla nel mio armadio. I ricordi tengono incatenate le persone. Ma che ne sai tu? Sei troppo giovane. Quanti anni hai… diciassette, diciotto?"

Il ragazzo tocca la giacca, ma non accenna a prenderla. "I ricordi, è questo che valgono per te… i dieci quindici dollari che puoi ricavare da qualcosa che lui portava addosso?"

"Senti," dice la donna. "Vai… vattene. Io devo mettere fuori le altre scatole. Adesso non ho tempo."

"Sì, il tempo, quando aspetti non passa mai. Lei ha sempre aspettato. Lui viaggiava per lavoro, e lei si fidava. Poi un giorno lui ha incontrato un'altra donna, e non è più tornato a casa."

"Senti, non so dove vuoi arrivare. Non sono cose che mi riguardano."

"Lui non te l'ha detto? Oh, no… e immagino che non l'hai mai chiesto… L'età dei figli… o quanti anni aveva il piccolo… non dico sua moglie."

"Non lo so chi sei… ma adesso prendi quella roba e vattene. E non tornare più!"

"Non lasciò un indirizzo, o qualche soldo per i figli… solo un biglietto."

Rabbiosamente, lei si asciuga gli occhi, si allontana.

"Mia madre non sa nemmeno che è già morto. Lo capisci questo?"

Lei si volta di scatto a guardarlo.

"Ma tu lo sai… e allora perché non glielo dici?"

"E tu che ne puoi sapere che significa perdere anche la speranza?"

La donna gli strappa la giacca di mano e la rimette sulla gruccia. "Se può farti piacere, lui teneva la tua foto nel portafoglio. Adesso so che sei tu. Un ragazzo, il minore."

"Già, un ragazzo."

"Posso andare a cercarla. È ancora da qualche parte nell'armadio." Comincia ad avviarsi verso la casa.

"Quanto vale?" dice lui, abbastanza forte per seguirla con la voce. "È per questo che non ci hai messo il prezzo, perché non lo sai, è così?"

Ma lei non si ferma. Entra e sbatte la porta dietro di sé.

Rimasto lì impalato, stringe a pugno la mano destra e colpisce con forza il palmo dell'altra mano. Poi, dopo un minuto, si decide a tornare alla macchina. Non c'è più niente che possa essere fatto. Ha speso i risparmi di due anni del suo magro salario per trovare suo padre... solo per sentirsi dire che era morto quattro mesi prima. L'investigatore privato aveva detto: "Mi dispiace, ragazzo, questa non ci voleva... Ma la donna con cui viveva ha organizzato una vendita di roba usata... forse può interessarti."

Mark guida lentamente fino alla fine della strada, una strada senza via d'uscita. Arrivato in fondo, gira. Ancora più lentamente ripassa davanti alla casa della donna. Dev'essere tornata indietro a prendere la giacca. Sta camminando verso la casa tenendola in mano.

Non la venderà più, se la terrà, ora ne è certo.

Era il modo in cui la teneva, stringendola a sé, che lo sorprese, quasi lo commosse. La rabbia che aveva dentro minacciava di dissolversi. Quella donna certo gli aveva voluto bene, a suo padre.

Continua a guidare. Ma dopo un po' è costretto ad accostarsi al lato della strada. Singhiozza. È tutto così inaspettato. Perché sto facendo così, pensa. Lui ci ha abbandonati... e allora perché sto piangendo come un bambino...? Mark però conosce la risposta. In fondo al cuore sa. Pensa alla giacca di pelle... alla donna. Non vedrà suo padre mai più. Mai più.

Ci vuole un po', ma poi i singhiozzi si placano. Si strofina la faccia con le mani. Gli occhi ora sono asciutti, ma il nodo dentro la gola fa male. Un dolore lancinante. E non sa come liberarsene.

## Note

1. The original story in English, "The Jacket," was published in *Sweet Lemons 2*, edited by Venera Fazio and Delia De Santis (Mineola, NY: Legas, 2010).

# America[1]

*Gil Fagiani*

Concetta lays out trays
of crushed tomatoes
to be dried on her fire escape.
She's making Sunday sauce
for her husband's family:
fifteen mouths of perpetual hunger.

Above Ninetta holds a spray bottle
her mother uses when ironing.
She sprays out the window,
watching droplets gleam in the sunlight,
laughs when a gust of wind blows
water in her face.

"*Hoooh! Assassino! Assassino!*"
Concetta bellows, as Ninetta's mother
runs into the room. "*Ch'è successo?*"
she says, sticking her head out the window.
"*My tomatoes are being ruined
by one of your brats,*" Concetta yells.

"*Mannaggia 'merica!*" – Damn America!
– Ninetta's mother cries.
*Why did my husband drag me
to this infernal place, far from
my village, with its soothing sounds
of sea waves and church bells,
its lemon orchards and honey lumps*

*of figs, away from papa and mamma,*
*my brother and sisters*

She stamps her feet, bites her knuckles,
grabs the bottle out of Ninetta's hands,
slapping her in the arms, face, legs,
leaving her to whimper all afternoon
in a corner of the hallway.

## Note

1. First published in *Feile-Festa: Literary Arts Journal* (Spring 2011).

# Concrete Porch, Iron Railings

*Frank Giorno*

Concrete porch
Iron railings
Metal bolts
Spiked and twisted nails
Aluminum screen doors
With the letter G
That once announced our name
Silhouettes of children once playing
Vapourized in time
Against back alley walls
The smell of mother's
Frittata, zucchini, eggplant with red pepper
Doused in garlic and blessed olive oil
Dissipated
Aromas now archived
In my memory along with
Drinking fathers in the underground cantina
While we the children played overhead
On the concrete porch with metal bolts and iron railings

# Poems from *Random Thoughts*[1]

*Marisa De Franceschi*

## Grandfathers

Mine had one leg missing.
Amputated well above the knee.
Gangrene.
That missing limb coaxed me across the ocean.
"I lost my limb, but got you back instead," he said.
I replaced the missing limb.
He tells me his missing limb hurts.
He can feel it, even though he sees it is not there.
"Just like you," he says.
"An ocean apart, but always in my heart."
"I'll miss you," he says,
"when you leave again.
The way I miss my missing limb."

"Your absence hurts."

## The Corkscrew Hazel Died This Year

The Corkscrew Hazel died this year.
For over thirty years its gnarled and twisted branches did their best,
Strained their necks to reach slivers of sun.
But you planted it too close to the house.
It bent over backwards to get out of its shade.
Alas, it has finally given up the battle and conceded defeat.
It dropped its leaves in Spring and no amount of coaxing could
Bring it back.
It was too late.

I look at my hands, my face, my back.
They too are gnarled and twisted. They too in pain from all the
Effort of trying to lean into you.
I bent myself to you, my sun God, but I too have reached too far
And feel ready to crack and give up the fight.

## The Threads that Bind

I sit outside in the morning sun
With a needle and thread and a pair of scissors.
I am snipping the stitching holding together the ticking
On my mother's pillows.
I need to bleach and wash the fabric.
She's been gone past a year now
And it's time I come to grips with some of her possessions.
Beneath the heavy cotton,
There is another, thinner lining encasing the feathers.
I'll leave that intact and wash it and the feathers together.
The plumes prick my fingers
And I am reminded of my grandmother.
It was her birds that contributed to these headrests.

I remember my mother performing this same ritual.
Snipping her mother's threads,
Then sewing everything up again.
I marvel at the neat and tidy stitches I am enravelling.
I will never be able to duplicate them.
I am not an agile seamstress.
Not good with a needle.
But I will do my best to put things back in order
And save the pillows for another night.
I lay the heavy cotton in the sun after I wash it.
When dry, I stitch it all back.
And when I do this, I realize
These are the threads that bind.

## Ironing Things Out

For me, it is satisfying to press clothes with a red, hot iron.
I smooth out folds and creases and feel in control.
I know I can scorch this fabric if I chose to
Or iron in new creases to annoy you.
Oh, yes, ironing can be a dangerous activity.
Left over anger can make my hand heavy
And I can pound the fabric and threaten its life.

But you are a clever lover.
You never fail to spritz yourself with scent,
Knowing it will escape from a shirt, or some other garment
To tantalize me.

My iron grip loosens,
The anger dissipates
As I iron things out.

## Svaporando stirando
*Translated by Maria Cristina Seccia*

A me dà soddisfazione premere sui vestiti con un ferro rosso, rovente.
Distendo le pieghe e le grinze e sento di avere controllo.
So che posso bruciare questo pezzo di stoffa se decido di farlo
O creare delle nuove grinze per infastidirti.
Ebbene sì, stirare può essere un'attività pericolosa.
La rabbia repressa può rendermi la mano pesante
E posso battere forte sul pezzo di stoffa e mettere in pericolo la sua vita.

Ma tu sei un amante furbo.
Non dimentichi mai di spruzzarti il profumo,
Sapendo che fuoriuscirà dalla maglietta, o da qualsiasi indumento
Per stuzzicarmi.

La presa del ferro si allenta.
La rabbia si dissipa
E svapora stirando.

## Note
1. Marisa De Franceschi, *Random Thoughts* (Montreal, Longbridge Books, 2010).

# In the Stacks[1]

*Licia Canton*

SHOULD I GRAB THEM ALL and have a seat at one of the tables, Rita wondered.

"Bagnell ... Harney...Iacovetta ... Ramirez ... Scarpaci...," she whispered.

The books were all on the same shelf at eye level. What luck. I won't have to roam about, she thought. And she wouldn't have to get the footstool. She hated getting up on that thing. She didn't have very good balance. It would be good to sit on it, though. Rita looked up and down the aisle to see if the stool was within reach.

She just wanted to look through the books. She wasn't sure she wanted to lug them all on the subway. She should have taken the car. It would have been easier on her back. But parking near the library was hard even at the end of the day. She didn't think there would be so many books to look through. Who would have thought, in a French university library. This is probably the last time I'll be here for a while, she thought.

She picked up Bagnell's *A Portrait of the Italian Canadians* and leafed through it. Rita had begun reading the introduction when she heard someone coming towards her.

"Excuse-moi," a man was trying to get past her.

"OK." She didn't look up. She moved over a bit but the man couldn't get through. She realized now how tight the aisle was and how wide she had become. He wasn't moving so she turned sideways.

"Sorry," Rita said in French. "Go ahead."

He moved over to the other side and then took a few steps back.

Rita continued reading Bagnell's book. She had read it years ago. She remembered. She had taken notes, but she might check it out of the library, she thought. They could ask her some historical questions. Rita wanted to be as prepared as possible even though she did not have a date yet. She did not want to waste any time. She had already wasted too much.

She picked up Ramirez's *The Italians of Montreal*. It was a dated book but still useful. And Ramirez taught in the history department at the university. She had never met him. He probably did not know about her research.

A light cough brought her back to the stacks. The man was still standing there. Not moving. She moved over slightly so he could reach the other shelves. He did not move.

Rita was uncomfortable with a man so close to her in the deserted library stacks. She remembered the man who had purposely stood behind her at the pharmacy while she pondered which brand to purchase. She had become increasingly nervous. She had walked out of the store without buying anything.

She turned around.

"Am I in your way?" she asked boldly.

He stood there tall, satchel in hand, leaning slightly against the stacks.

"J'attends," he grinned. "It's OK. Take your time. I'll wait."

"You are waiting for…?" She looked at him quizzically. "What?"

"I need those books." He indicated the shelf.

"Which ones?" she asked, hopeful that he wasn't referring to the ones she needed.

"All of them," he answered.

"Oh." She wasn't sure if he was serious or just toying with her. He wasn't making a pass at her, was he? That belly of hers was sure to keep men away for a while. But she was weary of French-speaking artsy types who smiled too easily.

"You're looking at the books on Italian immigration. Right?" he asked.

"Yes," she said firmly. "Do you need to take them out?"

"I'd like to. But first, I'd like to browse through them." He smiled again.

He will not get these books, she thought. He was too self-confident for her liking.

"You're Italian, aren't you?" He caught her off guard.

She didn't look Italian, she'd been told. Red hair and freckles. Maybe it was that maternal glow she had now which brought out her Italianness. Or maybe it was the protective way she held the books.

"You don't look Italian," he said, "but I can tell."

"Oh." Rita stared at his jean jacket.

"I can tell by your accent. You speak a polished, correct French with a very slight inflection. You're anglophone Italian. Am I right?" He was beaming. Waiting for confirmation.

Who is this québécois, she wondered, telling me I have an accent. She did have an accent, when she spoke French. And when she spoke English. And when she spoke Italian. She spoke properly, but in Québec, if you don't speak like a québécois, you have an accent.

"I'm a Montrealer. Born in Italy. Raised in an Italian family in the east end. Went to English school. Studied French at Marie Clarac. Spanish in college. German in Germany. I speak a Venetian dialect with my parents. Yes, I have an accent. Everyone does."

"I didn't ask for your CV," he chuckled. Then in a serious, kind voice: "I didn't want to offend you."

"No, of course not." It's the hormones, Rita said to herself.

"So where did the red hair come from? It's natural, right?"

"Now I could be offended by that," she smiled. "Do you know that there are twenty different regions in Italy? Do you know that not every Italian has dark hair and an olive complexion? Some are blond and have blue eyes or green eyes, and some have red hair like me."

"Of course I know that," he smiled.

"Oh?" Rita was intrigued.

"I know quite a bit about Italians. I'm from the east end, too."

"Oh."

"And my father is Italian," he grinned.

"Oh!"

"My name is Massimiliano." His pronunciation was perfect, mahs-see-mee-lee-ah-no but he put the accent on the o, as a francophone would. He looked québécois, he sounded québécois, but his name – a very long Italian name – was not a common one. This man was not a Tony, Frank or Joe.

She stared at him. He was not a Réal or Jean-Guy either.

Rita hadn't realized that she was hugging the books by Bagnell and Ramirez.

He smiled. He could tell she was confused.

"Nice to meet you," Massimiliano said, putting out his hand.

"Nice to meet you, too," Rita shifted the books and shook his hand. It was a genuine, firm handshake.

"My mother is a québécoise so I was raised in both cultures. But my father was the dominant force, of course. You know what I'm talking about, right? Italian men. Always right," he said. "I'm not like that."

She was surprised by his candour.

Italian men are all the same, she thought, whether they are born in Italy or not. She had stopped trying to convince herself otherwise.

"So you speak Italian then?" Rita asked.

"No, not at all."

His Italian father was the dominant force but he does not speak Italian, she thought. In all of her years at this university, all the hours she'd spent at the library, she had never seen him before. Where had he been hiding? This very québécois-looking, non-Italian speaking man, who had a very long name.

"So what do your friends call you?" she asked.

"Massimiliano," he said again with the accent on the o.

"I mean your francophone friends."

"I only have francophone friends ... that's the way it is since I work in a francophone milieu and I don't speak Italian and I am uncomfortable with English. They call me Massimiliano. Everyone does."

"Not Max or Maxime?" she insisted.

"No. Why?" he laughed. "Why would I change my name? My name is Massimiliano. I like it. It's not Guy or Jean."

"Interesting! How about your mom and your girlfriend? What do they call you?"

"Massimiliano, of course! I have a mom, but no girlfriend," he said smiling.

He's a funny guy, she thought.

"We can speak English. That way you can tell me if I have an accent," Rita suggested.

"But I said I don't speak English."

"You must speak a little," she was surprised.

"I understand, but I don't speak."

"Why not?"

"I don't like the language," he said bluntly.

"You're serious?"

"Yes. And I went to French school, raised in a French neighbourhood, work in a French office. No need to speak English. We're in Québec, remember?" He smiled again.

Oh no, so he is a *real* québécois, she thought. She did not want to get into a political debate.

"Yes. We're also in Canada," she smiled.

"Yes, but *I* live in Québec. Have you noticed that the signs are all in French?"

She sensed trouble looming in the next few minutes. She should just smile and leave it ...

"What are you doing waiting for these English books then?" She couldn't help herself.

"I said I don't speak English, but I can certainly read it." He wasn't smiling now.

She wasn't sure if he didn't speak or if he refused to speak.

"Books on the history of Italians ...," he said.

"Italians in *Canada*," she stressed.

"... for my thesis," he sighed. "My thesis is in anthropology. On Italians in Montreal ... Écoute," Massimiliano was not annoyed. "Listen. I don't want to put pressure on you so why don't we take all the books and sit at a table?"

Rita wasn't sure what to say.

"We can go through them and decide which we need," he said, looking at her belly. "Besides you must be getting tired, standing here."

"Yes, good idea. I *am* getting tired of standing," she said. "Thank you." She was glad the mood had changed.

He picked up all of the books on the shelf. "I'll carry these," he said.

She glared at him.

"Don't worry, I won't run off with them," he teased, as if he could hear her thoughts. "I'm a good québécois-Italian guy."

She followed him slowly down the aisle.

"When are you due?" he asked as they reached the tables. There were very few people around on a Thursday night.

"In about ten days."

"Wow, you must be quite the multi-tasker," he said amused. "One of those women who wants it all."

Rita wasn't sure what to say to that. Was he being complimentary or critical? Was he making fun of a pregnant graduate student?

"I want to get my thesis out of the way. Just polishing it up. Getting references, reading for the defence. I don't have a date yet but I want to read as much as possible before the baby comes."

"Is the father Italian too?"

"Yes. *He* is dark and olive-skinned. Born here of Italian parents and if anyone asks him where, he'll say he is from St. Leonard. Won't say he's Italian though. He's Montreal-born."

"Oh you are a St. Leo dame, too. Very, very Italian then."

"Well, I adopted St. Leonard. Don't get me confused with the stereotypes," she said. The words had slipped out too quickly.

"Stereotypes? My thesis is in anthropology, remember?"

They sat in front of each other for the next 45 minutes. He picked up one book at a time and wrote in his notebook. She read sections of Ramirez rapidly, worried that she might lose the book to the québécois anthropologist. She looked up at him every so often, and he smiled promptly every time. She was self-conscious, still unsure what to make of him.

He put the last book onto the pile on the table and put his notebook in his satchel. He waited for her to look up at him.

"I would ask you to join me for a coffee or a glass of wine, but you probably don't drink coffee or wine. And as a good Italian wife you will say "no" because hubby is waiting for you."

She smiled at the fact that this very un-Italian man had asked and answered for her. She looked at her watch.

"It's 7:30. I'd like to get home in time to put my twins to bed."

"Twins?"

"Yes, I have two little girls."

"Oh. This is your third child then?"

"Yes ...," she hesitated.

"An education and lots of children. Wow. A good little Italian girl." He wasn't teasing. His voice was serious, almost caring.

"Well ..."

"I was married once," his voice was sad. "Now at my age ... I look young, jean jacket and all, but I'm not. And I died many years ago when I lost her. I fell apart. I was so in love with her. I've only picked up my thesis again this year. I started it years ago. The therapy, the job ..."

She was touched by his openness. She did not want to interrupt him.

"Now I want to finish. Coming here brings me back. Meeting you, like this, unexpectedly ..." he sighed. "Sorry. I feel like I know you. I didn't mean to spill my whole story on you."

"Oh it's fine ... I ..." she paused.

"You have quite a bit of your own weight to carry," he chuckled. He was trying to get back into the happy-go-lucky guy she'd met in the stacks. "You can take the books. I've waited fifteen years to come back, I can wait a couple more weeks or months."

"Are you sure?" She was sincere. "I probably won't have time to read them all."

"You take them home," he insisted.

"Massimiliano," Rita said softly. "We all have our stories. It's not always as it seems. I fell in love with the wrong man ... And yes, now I am in a good place. But I know about therapy." Until then she had only ever said this to women.

"Give me your phone number and I will let you know when I bring the books back," she said warmly.

"Wow, a very pregnant, good Italian girl asking for my number!"

They laughed.

"I'm so happy to have met you," Massimiliano said, as he wrote his number on a scrap of paper. "I came over after work to look for books ... And it looks like I found a friend."

Rita reached over to take his number and smiled.

## Note

1. "In the Stacks" was first published in *Bridges: A Global Anthology of Short Stories*. Ed. Maurice A. Lee. Little Rock, AR: Tememos Publishing, 2012.

# Billy

## Michael Mirolla

BILLY (A NAME HE INFINITELY prefers to the Guglielmo given him at birth) has one leg shorter than the other, the result of an unfortunate encounter with a public transport vehicle. The mid-winter accident, leaving Billy trapped between the spinning back wheels and a hard-packed snow bank, couldn't have happened at a worst time. Billy was in the midst of undergoing some difficult hormonal changes and about to experience his first growth spurt. Although the spurt arrived on time, it only took hold of the upper half of his body, giving him the look of a bandy-legged, weightlifting rooster. And that, as a rule, could be more than ample reason for pity - or derision. That could be the signal to take the luckless victim under society's wing, to relegate him to that area where "tut-tut" is the operative word most often heard. This is especially true when the person happens to be a second-generation immigrant. But no one sighs or laughs or "tut-tuts" when Billy ambles by, his misstep making it appear as if he can't decide what height he really wants to be. No one chooses to point him out with a wiggling finger or to express open sympathy with his plight. No one comments on his status as an abandoned youth or as one of life's incompletely-formed. And certainly no one says that Billy should be in some sort of institution - at least, no one says it out loud. No one says it in his presence. For, you see, any or all of the above options would hurt Billy's sensibilities - and that, in turn, wouldn't be very healthy for those exercising said options.

Despite the asymmetry - or because of it, Billy takes great pleasure in dressing in his finest duds and strolling the streets. "His" streets, having returned to claim uncontested ownership not long after his final graduation from the Shawbridge Farm and Reformatory School for Wayward Boys. Occasionally and for no particular reason, he stops, sticks his hands into his specially-made silk trouser pockets and broods. More often, he simply concentrates on forcing himself not to smile, in keeping with his serious, if somewhat self-imposed, responsibilities. When he does choose to focus on someone, look out. It's as if the rifles from a firing squad had suddenly been primed. Some might be tempted to say that behind that hooded, lizard stare lies spread the deadly history of Park Extension, of misinterpreted New World dreams and rough woollen underwear that hasn't been changed quite often enough. Or that has been worn threadbare from too many direct applications of javel water. Some might be tempted to say that - despite the fact Billy's own underwear is always of the finest weave and never has to be worn more than once. But no one would. And how Billy has managed to go from abandoned childhood to personal tailor is another question that's best left unexplored.

Billy cherishes his independence, his freedom to do as he pleases when he pleases. He lives by himself in a pleasant but modest two-room flat above an Armenian grocery store-cum-dentist office. This flat had once housed his mother as well but she opted out of the lease soon after Billy's accident (his father having opted out long before that, cursing the land repeatedly as the boat headed back to the Old Country). As far as anyone can tell, he has lived by himself ever since - when, that is, not taking part in one of his sporadic reform school apprenticeships. And he has made it known, forcibly at times, that this is the condition he prefers, that he doesn't care for anyone and isn't interested in sharing the occasional heart-to-heart the rest of us find so soothing. Never has, never will. In fact, his favourite expression - and this from a young man of very few words - is: "I couldn't give a flying mother about youse. Get outta my face." Which freely translated means: Avoid the dapper gentleman for the foreseeable future or you won't have much of a future to foresee.

But only his "friends" does he treat in such a chivalrous and courtly manner. As for his enemies, they receive no warning. None whatsoever. Often, by the time they find out about their ill-fated change in status, it's too late. Way too late. One moment, they're walking along a sunset-cloaked Park Ex street, whistling with youthful exuberance and without a care in the world after a visit with an accommodating signorina; the next, they're laid out expeditiously and efficiently, contemplating the dizzy, eternal round of stars from a dark pool of their own vital fluid. At which point, Billy might lean down and offer a helping hand. He might deign to explain what brought on the "lesson" in the first place and why it was deemed necessary. Or he might not.

And God help anyone crazy enough to disturb the calm of what Billy sweetly refers to as "home away from home." That's the far-wall, facing-the-door booth at the Nero's Palace night club where he sits for hours on end surrounded by a revolving cast of his favourites (always male), each bringing in a tithe or a trinket from their far-flung business activities. Chances are said disturbers, by definition strangers to the area who don't know any better and haven't taken proper heed of the danger signals, will soon be flying through picture windows one step ahead of a shotgun blast. On most occasions, Billy will take care to shoot well over their heads - but there's no telling when he won't. No telling when he might feel compelled to lower his aim. And then calmly walk away, leaving enough money to cover the shattered pane and a round for those with the courage to have stuck it out.

But what Billy enjoys best, what brings a spark into the perennial dull of his eyes, is a punishment he reserves for only the most heinous of crimes: a punishment that involves jumping from the tops of fences. Fences not too high and not too low; fences with just the right footholds; fences with the proper give and take. And then landing with a delicious thud on the chest of his laid-out victim, pinned down below with uncaring yet casual effectiveness by Billy's Hounds.

Billy's Hounds are his ace retrievers. He, himself, due to the previously-mentioned lack of symmetry, can't run with any competence. Besides, such precipitous motion would be a gross indignity, an admitting of undue haste and concern when those words don't exist in Billy's vocabulary. But his retrievers, also reform-school trained, are the finest in all of Park Ex. Always hungry, lithe, lean and long of limb, breathlessly swift and guaranteed not to injure the prey. In short, they're exemplary hounds, recruited with just one purpose in mind. Nothing can divert them or lead them astray: neither family loyalty, nor "agenbites of inwit." A false trail, an attempt to dodge down some garbage-strewn alley, will most certainly prove useless: Billy's Hounds know every street, every dead-end, every abandoned building, garage and construction site in Park Ex. And a plea for mercy only excites them the more, only leads them to snigger and nod knowingly, all the while closing in with military precision. A sudden turn, a snarl, a show of teeth and knotted fists has the best effect - causing them to stop in their tracks. But only for a moment. For they're quick to recover - more fearful of returning empty-handed than of any damage the quarry might be able to inflict.

Once surrounded and caught, once made to understand there's no escape, once led to the point of no return (normally at the base of the chain-link metal fence that runs along the railroad track), the victim's waiting must be a terrible, excruciating agony. Billy's slow side-tilted gait becomes even more pronounced at such times. He will stop occasionally - like a man in love - to crack his knuckles. Or to suck on a minted toothpick. Or to comb his Brillantined hair. Or to adjust the buttons on his dapper double-breasted suit. As he resumes his walk, a cold somewhat cynical moon gleams back from his newly-shined footwear. For he always detours through the railroad station concession to have his boots polished to a sparkle before a "kill." And he smiles. Now he smiles. At last he smiles. Such a smile is hard to imagine, quite impossible to re-create in any believable way. You need a dark as dark as a soul never given a chance, a soul crushed beyond recognition under the relentless tires of a winter bus. And then you need to sprinkle this dark with just the right amount of emptiness, a little soupçon of nothing like the cursed wake of a retreating ghost ship.

Following the jingle up the chain-link fence (not too high, not too low), Billy's downward flight is a thing of infinite beauty, of perfect arc, of ultra-accurate trajectory: a rainbow with every single colour rubbed out save the red. It's all the more fascinating in that, on the way down, one boot is necessarily ahead of the other - for a double thunk. A thu-thunk. And, if you listen carefully enough, if you put your mind to it, you can hear Billy's delighted "wheeee!" as he allows gravity to mete out justice for him. Only once has he missed beneath the shadow of that concrete overpass into Park Ex - and that was definitely towards excess. With a crushed skull, a careering ambulance ride, a critical listing, the result.

It's only after such punishments that Billy allows himself a few laughs, that Billy lets his guard down. Then - in the familiar surroundings of his "home" and circumscribed by his faithful Hounds, each one vying for a pat on the head or a word of praise - he opens up and begins to talk. What's more, he allows others to talk, those with infinitely better verbal skills and memories, those with a gift for gab. For Billy isn't afraid to admit his own deficiencies when it comes to such matters - as long as no one else does. The talk is of exploits and brave deeds, of the good old days at the reform school, of escapes attempted and escapes succeeded. Anything goes, provided the evening ends with a re-cap of Billy's own accomplishments and a re-affirming of his value to the community.

But one mustn't get the impression Billy's life is all peaches and cream, all sweetness and light. Sometimes his enemies, envious of his success, will stage a pre-emptive strike deep into his staked-out territory, causing havoc among Billy's business associates and appropriating their hard-earned goods. Sometimes, emboldened by grief or blinded by revenge, the brother or the cousin or the long-time friend of the crushed skull will blast away the picture window of Billy's "home" and then retreat to the far side of the railroad overpass, safe in the womb of another language, another night. And sometimes, there's even a certain tit-for-tat, with one of Billy's Hounds tossed off the same railroad bridge - to scream and flail and suffer a shattered spine on the unforgiving tracks below.

On such occasions, there's no talking to Billy. No point in even trying. A pure madness invades his eyes. It's a clean devoid-of-life madness. It's a madness that allows him to stash a machine-gun under his spotless, recently dry-cleaned trench coat. That allows him to stand vigil all night over "his" end of the bridge, the one necessary gap in an otherwise impenetrable armour. No doubt dangerous and exposed, if someone doesn't know his enemies. But Billy knows them intimately, knows them as he knows himself. Better, really. For he's had plenty of occasion to deal with them.

Come on, he will say, legs apart and well-balanced, machine-gun held loosely in one hand. Come to me, youse bleeding mothers, he will say while his Hounds wait curled up and whimpering at the base of the overpass. Come on. Here I am. Come and get me. And, unable to help themselves, his enemies will begin their long sojourn from the well-guarded halls of warmth and protection, from the arms of their girlfriends, from the pool room basements full of dusty light, from the 24-hour snack bars redolent with the smell of vinegar and ketchup. Clomp, clomp, clomp, marching in orderly phalanxes up the cement ramp, up the crumbling steps, drawn by the absolute magnet of Billy's hate. They march and they fall, blown away by the steady blissful rat-a-tat that blazes like a single red-hot eye from somewhere close to Billy's heart.

And then they march and they fall again - and again after that, the entire night long. And for every single night after that. Tireless. Unconcerned with the niceties of time and plans for the future. They march and fall again as often as Billy calls them - and that could be a long, long time.

You see, neither simple death nor the promise of subsequent resurrection is enough for Billy. It has never been enough. Not nearly enough.

It's the again and again that comes closest to satisfying his soul. It's the stiff blast of eternity he seeks out. A relentless pursuit for release.

In the fervent hope that, someday, his enemies will do the same for him.

# Part III

# Past, Present and the Hybrid Self
## *Critical and Creative Considerations*

# Transcultural Creative Non-Fiction: Caterina Edwards' *Finding Rosa* and Janice Kulyk Keefer's *Honey and Ashes*. Finding the Way Home Through Narrative

*Maria Tognan*

IN THIS PAPER, I DRAW a parallel between Janice Kulyk Keefer's *Honey and Ashes* and Caterina Edwards' *Finding Rosa* in order to cast light on the ways in which transcultural creative non-fiction became for both authors the elected medium to write, and therefore find, their way home. *Honey and Ashes* was published in 1998, while *Finding Rosa* appeared ten years later, in 2008. However, neither time nor differences in ethnic background need prevent the drawing of a parallel between the works of these two authors in search of a deeper understanding of their identity, because, even though driven by different needs, both writers chose to piece together family narratives and to connect them to collective history in order to bring home a new, rediscovered, sense of self. Kulyk Keefer's and Edwards' are works of highly emotional creative non-fiction which foreground historical and personal reflection through a balanced mixture of travel writing, biography, memoir and imaginative reconstruction, in a powerful combination made possible by an acute meta-narrative awareness. Far from trying to simplistically level out their differences, I wish to compare and contrast aspects of writing ethnicity, memory and imagination in the works under scrutiny, seeking to distil such elements not into a paradigm but into a host of comparable transcultural processes which underlie the understanding of ethnic identity. After providing the background to Edwards' and Kulyk Keefer's respective works of creative non-fiction, I intend to outline a framework for the ideas of transculturalism and creative non-fiction, in order to clarify how the authors exploited the possibilities of this hybrid genre to map the neighbouring terrains of memory and identity in their private and collective (and therefore cultural) aspects. Finally, I will argue that the authors described how they found their way home by means of writing, and also that the process of writing itself became their way home in that it contributed to the creation of a narrative scaffolding for identity.

Kulyk Keefer and Edwards are two prolific writers who have explored the issues of ethnicity both in fictional and creative non-fictional works. Kulyk Keefer was born in Toronto from a mixed Ukrainian and Polish background. She grew up, and currently lives, in Canada, although she also spent part of her life in England, where she had moved for her graduate studies, and in France (Kulyk Keefer, "Coming Across Bones" 85-88; "Janice Kulyk Keefer Interviewed" 188). Edwards was born in England and currently lives in Edmonton. Her background is also mixed: her father, Frank, was English and her mother, Rosa Pagan, was born in Lussino (now Lošinj), an island in the Adriatic Sea, characterized in the past by a troubled political history (cf. Edwards, *Finding Rosa*; Caterinaedwards.com). Edwards' family migrated to Canada when she was eight years old.

In the 1990s Kulyk Keefer travelled to Ukraine to carry out research for *The Green Library*, a novel which was published in 1996, and later to investigate her ethnicity and her family history. Her endeavours in this direction led her to write *Honey and Ashes – A Story of Family*. As Kulyk Keefer explained in her essay "Coming Across Bones: Historiographic Ethnofiction" (1995), even if for some time she had distanced herself from, and even repudiated, her ethnicity, she finally claimed that baggage and engaged in writing ethnicity to conceptualize her "hyphenated state" in terms other than those of "two discrete ethnic or national identities" (87). Throughout Kulyk Keefer's childhood, the narratives of life in her mother's village had formed "a third terrain, even a home ground of imagination" which she could enter effortlessly "without the shameful clumsiness marking those shifts from 'Ukrainian' to 'English' spheres" that she associated with Canada (88). As she stated in *Honey and Ashes*, for her, travelling "back" to Ukraine meant returning somewhere she had never been (215; cf. "Coming across Bones" 94). There she experienced first hand the hardships of the land, the gap between the real Ukraine and the imagined one, and the troubling sensation of being at once a native, or at least an envoy, and a tourist (*Honey and Ashes* 244 *et passim*; cf. Grekul 147).

Similar feelings with regard to identity are effectively expressed by Edwards on her website, in which she states that the opportunity she had in her youth to spend the summer holidays with her mother's family in Venice, and to experience the contrast in cultures, made her realize that "identity is not fragmentary but multiple" (*Caterinaedwards.com*). *Finding Rosa* is the result of a research into the culture which shaped Rosa Pagan (261), carried out in order to understand the kind of upbringing the writer received from her. Edwards is part of that "sandwich generation" of women, caught between providing for children and caring for ailing parents and in-laws ("Finding Rosa – Paperback" *Dmpibooks.com*): as the subtitle to the book – *A Mother with Alzheimer's, a Daughter in Search of the Past* – clarifies, her project was an attempt to counteract the consequences of her mother's condition (which leads to memory loss) through writing. At the same time, it was an endeavour to inscribe her own identity by defining it in relationship to (and possibly against) that of her mother. In an interview with Sabrina Francesconi, Edwards declared:

> She lost her memories and she gradually lost herself. At the time, in trying to understand the process, I started to think of the concept of lost memories and lost histories ... I was interested ... in the way we recreate the past through writing. I tried to recreate my mother's life through my imagination. But of course the result is my construction. (Francesconi, "Constructing Memories" n. pag)

As Edwards states on her website, the writing of *Finding Rosa* originated from the need to piece together family history to arrive at the roots of her sense of never belonging. Unlike Kulyk Keefer, Edwards had travelled to Istria and Italy before the journey of 2001 described in *Finding Rosa*. However, in her memoir, she confessed that throughout her youth she had perceived her mother's past as "hazy and ... irrelevant" (29): "Istria was a fantasy, a mental construct, a sequence of images incubated by my dreams. It existed in my mother's mind [...] as the beloved, lost homeland, the wellspring of nostalgia" (29). Edwards set out to research the past of Istria to discover which historical events had affected her mother's family directly, and thus arrived at the roots of her mother's often difficult behaviour (*Finding Rosa* 291) and finally managed to forgive her (Personal Interview).[1]

Different as the needs which drove Kulyk Keefer's and Edwards' investigations are, it is still possible to detect a resemblance in the authors' wish to achieve a geo-political, historical and personal knowledge of their "homelands" and share it through narrative. During their journeys, both writers faced the difficulty of reconstructing their family history in places where historical evidence was scanty, since masses of people had been deported or forced to leave, and archives had been conveniently destroyed as a consequence of wars and violent political instability. Furthermore, Kulyk Keefer and Edwards were confronted with the fact that some of their relatives were reluctant or unable to share stories from a past so strongly marked by suffering. The memories they were trying to put together proved to be subjective, selective, decaying, even unreliable – although unwittingly so. In the process of recuperating family stories and connecting them to one another, as well as to collective history, both writers experienced and re-discovered the value of memory by measuring it against its absence. As a consequence, in the books under scrutiny, the scantiness of evidence, the limited number of documents, and the defectiveness of memory are counterbalanced by imagination.

The imaginative reconstruction of the past, fuelled by stories passed on by family members, constitutes relevant portions of both *Honey and Ashes* and *Finding Rosa*. In Kulyk Keefer's and Edwards' works of creative non-fiction, the entwining of memory and imagination results in compelling narratives which reach out to the "old country" to foreground, in Kulyk Keefer's words, that "continuum of experience, and, most of all, imagination that can bring us all, however momentarily, together" (*Honey and Ashes* 7). Writing creative non-fiction to bridge a cultural gulf between the present and the past, between Canada and the country of origin, becomes for the authors a way to perceive the weight exerted by history on their ethnicity and their identity. Edwards writes: "The dynamic of memory and stories is that of two glowing ropes that intertwine and separate, slip by each other and knot over the dark pit, the *foiba* of forgetfulness" (*Finding Rosa* 176). As a remedy to a worrying collective tendency to the oblivion and denial of uncomfortable historical truths, the writers' family memories are shared through the same means they were received: narratives in which the human side to historical events emerges from the intersection between the personal and the collective; a result which could not be achieved by means of historical writing alone. The skilfully woven narratives by Kulyk Keefer and Edwards expound historical information in a form which fosters the emotional response of the reader, enabling him to relate to individual destinies singled out from, and conjured out of, the anonymous multitudes of collective history.

The choice of "creative non-fiction" as a genre does not entail the authorial decision to give free rein to imagination, embellishing fact with invention. According to Judy O'Malley, the cardinal rule of creative non-fiction is "[n]ever lie: [i]f you made up some of the elements, bring your reader into that process: use an author's note to explain clearly what, why, and where" (qtd. in Taylor Brown n. pag.). In fact, both Kulyk Keefer and Edwards, by means of different devices or meta-narrative choices, make the reader aware of their authorial insertions. Kulyk Keefer, for instance, declares in her prologue to *Honey and Ashes* that "what memory hides and what imagination discloses" (5) are all part of the book she has written; and later reminds the reader, in the acknowledgements section, that "the turns given to these stories, and the inevitable errors that have crept into the telling are [hers] alone" (330). Although Edwards is more substantial in her semi-fictional reconstructions, she also makes them overtly recognizable. To quote just one example from *Finding Rosa*, in Chapter 8, "Who remembers?", the writer reconstructs a trip to the *piazza* which little Rosa took with her father, narrating it in a voice which reproduces the little girl's thoughts, and is therefore markedly different from the main one.

Both authors underline the inextricability of memory and imagination. Edwards declared in the interview with Francesconi that memory and imagination are entwined, explaining that memories of the past change, they are constructed, and yet they are "essential to our creating a narrative, an understanding of our world." In addition, in a personal interview, Edwards described the way in which she perceives memory to be connected to imagination, saying that when you think back on your life you remember certain details, but you also imagine and recreate them in a process which involves fictionalization. She then paralleled such a process to what happens in creative non-fiction, that is, that fictional narrative strategies are employed in order to produce a story that is connected to one's personal construction of reality. Similarly, also in a personal interview, Kulyk Keefer explained that there is "no such thing as pure memory," because "it always emerges as story," and added that since it is inherent in human beings to remember in narrative form, imagination inevitably inserts itself in the process. Therefore, all one can do is "test" that what one has "superimposed" such as a metaphor or a correlative, is as "fitting,... resonant" and "as truthful as it could possibly be."[2]

In light of these considerations, it becomes clear that the reader of creative non-fiction should take the stories told by the writers not as objective truth, but as an imaginative reflection of it, linguistically engendered in a subjective mind and therefore by no means less *true*. In other words, the truth of creative non-fiction is the truth each author has unearthed for herself digging through archives, memories and family narratives; the truth on or against which each of them will base any further understanding of her self image. The empowering value of narrative lies in the fact that the authors can accommodate in it a sense of belonging which is at once real and imagined. Narrating their family stories enabled them to, in words borrowed from Pier Aldo Rovatti, "*accettare la sfida di una identità senza luogo, disegnando i contorni di una prossimità esposta al fuori e all'alterità ma non cancellata da questa esposizione*" (29).[3] In both *Honey and Ashes* and *Finding Rosa*, what is at stake is the construction of an identity and of an idea of home which are supported by the scaffolding of narrative and writing. Peter Brooks, in *Reading for the Plot* wrote: "Our lives are ceaselessly intertwined with narrative, with the stories that we tell and hear told... all of which are reworked in that story of our own lives that we narrate to ourselves in a virtually uninterrupted monologue" (3). In *Finding Rosa* Edwards confessed that, before she could write words down, she told herself stories, and identified her storytelling with the need to create a space for herself by erecting a wall against her mother, especially in times of transition (247). *Finding Rosa* ends with a passage in which Edwards thinks back to the time she received a blessing from her mother. To speak about it, the writer alludes to the Biblical image of Jacob, who fought with the angel and hung on until he received his blessing. Edwards hung on, she explains, not just until she received the blessing but until she *knew* her mother – a knowledge she achieved by writing the book (*Finding Rosa* 334). Interestingly, in her 2004 paper "Wrestling with the Angel, the Self and the Publisher in Life Writing" (27), Edwards compared the process of writing to wrestling with the angel, alluding to the same Biblical reference (and to Virginia Woolf). In writing *Finding Rosa*, the effort made to be blessed as a daughter and as a writer, the processes of getting to know her mother and of writing about it, took place simultaneously, both struggles a contribution to shaping Edwards' identity as a woman, a mother and a writer (cf. *Finding Rosa* 127).

As to Kulyk Keefer, she declared in *Coming Across Bones* that the most important, yet invisible, component of her ethnicity was something she never could or wanted to shake off: "the component of story, the narratives my grandmother, mother, and aunt would tell me all through my childhood and adolescence." In the same essay and in her novel *The Green Library*, to convey the ambivalent experience of ethnic identity in a visual way, Kulyk Keefer employed the image of double-faced Janus, the Roman god of thresholds, implying that ethnicity signifies looking at the same time in the direction of the old and the new country. As Grekul aptly summarized, Kulyk Keefer in her 1991 essay *From Mosaic to Kaleidoscope* argued that, as opposed to multiculturalism, transculturalism reflects more accurately "the day-to-day realities of individuals from ethnic minority backgrounds, many of whom harbour strong material and/or emotional attachments to their ancestral homelands" (Grekul 111). Furthermore, Deborah Saidero, in "Janice Kulyk Keefer's Transcultural Transcodifications" explained:

> Keefer [...] postulates the construction of a post- or transnational identity, wherein immigrants can develop a sense of belonging to their Canadian homeland without denying their other homes in the process. This new concept entails a reconfiguration of the idea of "home," which becomes an imaginative space that transcends political and geographical confines, a space where history, memory and place cohabit and intermingle (110).

Kulyk Keefer's and Edwards' works of creative non-fiction are therefore transcultural in that they satisfy the need to create a connection to the respective "old countries" in an effort to understand and embrace one's cultural background, and also in that they fulfil the need to bear witness and keep memories alive for the sake of later generations. Writing plays a paramount role in the process of re-imagining the authors' sense of self and community, which together comprise the ideas of home and identity. The two authors exploit the hybrid genre of creative non-fiction to depict within its blurred boundaries, "the jumble of the individual and the universal" (the words are Edwards', from her website). To summarize, the choice of creative non-fiction as the means to merge the results of research with the fragments offered by family history, is significant in many respects: first of all, it allowed the writers to fill in the gaps created by the selectivity of subjective memory or by the intentional and more or less extensive obliteration of collective memory operated by historical agents; secondly, it helped to foreground the role of narrative in providing a scaffolding for the ideas of identity and home, and finally, it proved ideal for depicting what Kulyk Keefer calls "this world that's mine by inheritance and imagination" (*Honey and Ashes* 202), an ethnicity defined at once by fact and by family myth.

To conclude, I would like to make reference to a few lines from "Homecoming," the epilogue to *Honey and Ashes*, in which Kulyk Keefer weighs up a dictionary definition of the word "home" against her own appraisal of the notion:

> Home, as the dictionary defines it, a 'fixed dwelling-place, one's habitual or proper abode.... A place, region or state to which one properly belongs, in which one's affections centre, or where one finds rest, refuge or satisfaction. One's own country, one's native land, the place where one's ancestors dwelt.' Yet even as I read this litany of definitions, the conflicts and contradictions leap up at me. Rest, refuge, satisfaction – none of these fit what I feel about Staromischyna, or about the Ontario to which I have returned. Perhaps home is only this: inhabiting uncertainty, the arguments desire picks with fear (328).

Uncertainty lingers because books of creative non-fiction are "books that are open-ended, asking as many questions as they attempt to answer, demonstrating that we are constantly expanding, re-assessing, and gaining new understanding of who we are and what we know" (O'Malley, qtd. in Taylor Brown n. pag.). This is especially true of *Finding Rosa* and *Honey and Ashes*. Both Edwards' and Kulyk Keefer's writing of their way home can now be described as twofold: on the one hand, through writing they *describe how* they found their way home (the difficulty, the research, the discoveries); on the other, the process of writing itself *becomes* their way home by being the force which holds the jigsaws of awareness together, finally giving coherence and meaning to their journeys, and preparing them for new ones (cf. *Honey and Ashes* 329 *et passim*).

## Notes

1. Used with permission.

2. Used with permission.

3. To "accept the challenge of an identity without dwelling, drawing the contours of a proximity exposed to the outside and to alterity, although not wiped out by such exposition" [My translation].

## Works Cited

Brooks, Peter. *Reading for the Plot: Design and Intention in Narrative*. 1984. Cambridge, MA: Harvard UP, 1992. Print.

Donovan, Melissa. "Creative Nonfiction." *Writingforward.com*, 2010: n. pag. Web. 19 May 2010. <http://www.writingforward.com/category/genres/creative-nonfiction>.

Edwards, Caterina. *Finding Rosa: A Mother with Alzheimer's, a Daughter in Search of the Past*. Vancouver: Greystone Books 2008. Print.

\_\_\_\_\_. "Wrestling with the Angel, the Self and the Publisher in Life Writing." *Shaping History: L'Identità Italo-Canadese nel Canada Anglofono*. Vol. 1. Eds. Anna Pia De Luca and Alessandra Ferraro. Proceedings of the International Conference *Oltre la Storia / Beyond History / Au delà de l'Histoire: L'Identità Italo-Canadese Contemporanea*," 20-22 May 2004, Udine. Udine: Forum 2005. 23-30. Print.

\_\_\_\_\_. "Finding Rosa – Paperback." *Dmpibooks.com*. 2008-2010 Web. 19 May 2010. <http://dmpibooks.com/book/finding.rosa-paperback>.

Francesconi, Sabrina. "Constructing Memory Through Imagination. An Interview with Caterina Edwards." *Bibliosofia: Letteratura Canadese e Altre Culture/Canadian Literature and Other Cultures*. Ed. Egidio Marchese. *Bibliosofia.net*, 21 May 2004: n. pag. Web. 14 Apr. 2009. <http://www.bibliosofia.net/files/Sab.htm>.

Grekul, Lisa. *Leaving Shadows: Literature in English by Canada's Ukrainians*. Edmonton: U of Alberta Press, 2005. Print.

Kulyk Keefer, Janice. "Coming Across Bones: Historiographic Ethno-fiction." *Essays on Canadian Writing* 57 (Winter 1995): 84-104. Print.

\_\_\_\_\_. *Honey and Ashes: A Story of Family*. Toronto: Harper Collins, 1998. Print.

\_\_\_\_\_. "From Mosaic to Kaleidoscope: Out of the Multicultural Past Comes a Vision of a Transcultural Future." *Books in Canada* 20.6 (Sept. 1991): 13-16. Print.

\_\_\_\_\_. "Janice Kulyk Keefer Interviewed by Cherry Clayton." *The Journal of Commonwealth Literature* 34.1 (1999): 183-197.

Marchese, Egidio. "Presentiamo Caterina Edwards." *Bibliosofia: Letteratura Canadese e Altre Culture/Canadian Literature and Other Cultures*. Ed. Egidio Marchese. *Bibliosofia.net*, 1 April 2006: n. pag. Web. 14 Apr. 2009. <http://www.bibliosofia.net/files/presentiamo_caterina_edwards.htm>.

McCrary, Micah. "Creative Nonfiction: In Defense of the Truth (with a Lower Case T)." *Bookslut* 95 (April 2010): n. pag. Web. 19 May 2010. <http://www.bookslut.com/features/2010_04_016065.php>.

Pivato, Joseph, ed. *Caterina Edwards: Essays on Her Works*. Toronto: Guernica, 2000. Print.

Rovatti, Pier Aldo. *Possiamo Addomesticare l'Altro? La Condizione Globale*, Udine: Forum, 2007. Print.

Saidero, Deborah. "Janice Kulyk Keefer's Transcultural Transcodifications." *Reading Janice Kulyk-Keefer*. Ed. Deborah Saidero. Udine: Forum, 2009. 105-116. Print.

Taylor Brown, Susan. "Creative Nonfiction: a True Story Well Told." 2004. *Susantalyorbrown.com*, 2005: n. pag. Web. 19 May 2010. <http://www.susantaylorbrown.com/creativenf.html>.

Tognan, Maria. Personal Interview with Caterina Edwards. Unpublished. 28 April 2009.

_____. Personal Interview with Janice Kulyk Keefer. Unpublished. 18 May 2009.

# Reverse Translation

*Darlene Madott & Gianna Patriarca*

(*On the publication, in Italian, of Gianna Patriarca's* Donne Italiane ed Altre Tragedie)

GIANNA PATRIARCA WAS BORN IN Ceprano, Frosinone in 1951. She came to Canada in 1960, as a child, along with her mother and younger sister, to join her father who had emigrated four years earlier. She graduated from York University with a degree in English Literature and Italian and a B. Ed. Now retired, she taught for the Toronto Catholic District School Board for over thirty years. Gianna has written and published numerous books of poetry, a book for children, and has read her work in Canada, the USA and Italy. Her award-winning first book, *Italian Women and Other Tragedies,* was translated into Italian in 2009, and is available from LyricalMyrical Press in Toronto.

I first encountered Gianna on the television. We were both women in our thirties at the time. Gianna was speaking about life in Little Italy, around Clinton and College. An imposing, expressive woman, with blood-red lipstick and red nails, and mass of dark, curly hair, she leapt out of the television screen and into my living room. She was the first voice I heard, quintessentially Italian and Canadian – a woman. I don't remember what she said that day, but I do remember how it made me feel – not so alone, and joyous.

What follows are excerpts from an interview I conducted with Gianna, on the occasion of the publication of her first book translated into the Italian language. We started our interview in the kitchen of her home, and continued at a local restaurant at the corner of Grace and College, in Little Italy, Toronto. The interview excerpts are "laced" with four poems, which were read, firstly in the Italian, and then in English, at the conference proceedings in Atri, Abruzzo, June 2010.

**How involved were you in the translation process? Can you tell us about your choice of work to be translated? Why this book, to be the first?**

I was right there with the translation, back and forth through emails and attachments. If it didn't have the essence, spirit or soul that had been the original then I'd work on it along with the translator Maria Grazia Nalli (she's a second cousin and close friend). After Maria Grazia and I had completed the translation, I passed it on to three people whose Italian is stronger than mine, to check it out for me – people who were close to and respectful of the work (Corrado Paina, Father John Carparelli, and Professore Gianni Blasi). When you are translating literature, what you say is as important as how you say it, so it is a delicate exercise.

I have Grade 3 in Italian, so I found it challenging and fun to translate my own work but it was not easy. Part of the process of this work: I read a lot of people in translation – Neruda, Pasolini, Rocco Scotellaro, Nazim Hikmet, Primo Levi and others, a lot of poets from around the world that I can only read in translation. Often I found some translations touch you more than others. For instance, the Italian, I can read and see what's happening in the style and choice of words, but with Spanish or Turkish or Russian, for example, I have to rely completely on the translation. If the translation moves me, allows me to feel what the poem is about, then I know it is a pretty good translation.

I think we get bogged down sometimes, with things having to fit into some kind of formula or order. I believe that language should be free, especially when writing poetry – express it in different ways, even if it doesn't fit the format of the so-called proper language. Italians can be a little uptight about using the proper and polite form, they have a way of making you feel inadequate – *oh, you can't say it that way or you must use it this way* – I find that so limiting. Yes I can; I can say it any way I want, and I will.

One of the people who read my translation (who will remain unnamed) said that it didn't meet the standards of proper Italian, and that it needed a lot of work, because the Italians would "laugh me out of the country" with my translation. It upset me, but I took it with a grain of salt. I knew that this person had lost sight of the poetry, the message, the meaning, but was concentrating on the *figura* of the language.

My poetry isn't about the *figura*, the standard beautiful Italian language: it's about reaching a place where you may have to go through the back door, and not the front door to reach. It is about language in transition, a language that doesn't stay put but moves and changes because of the influence of many things: place, time, migration, integration, and on and on... *Donne Italiane ed Altre Tragedie* will always be a kind of experimental translation. These poems were not born in Italian. But I am very pleased they are living in my Italian.

Poems can only live completely in one language and often lose something when they are translated into another. It's like an original and a print. You can look at them and they're both beautiful but there's something that can never be fully captured in the print. Maybe the energy between the hand and the brush, the pen and the fingers... who knows?

When something is born in one way – it is original. You can make a million copies in different ways and they can be totally engaging, but they can't be the original.

RITORNARE

*non discutiamo più la distanza*
*ritornare adesso è*
*l'altro sogno*
*niente affatto Americano*
*nè Canadese nè Italiano*
*ha perso la sua nazionalità*

*negli anni sessanta arrivammo a sciami*
*come le api d'estate*
*emanando uno strano odore*
*indossando l'ultimo bacio umido*
*del nostro cielo*
*arrivammo con bauli pesanti*
*tasche vuote*
*e un sogno.*

*ero una di loro*
*nascosta sotto la linea del mare*
*nella carena d'una nave*
*che si gonfiava e svuotava*
*per tredici giorni*

*le nostre pance*
*sull'Atlantico*
*finché la nave finalmente ci vomitò*
*sulla riva di Halifax*
*dove le braccia e le gambe*
*della mia bambola si staccarono*
*e caddero nel mare*
*ritornando a casa sulle onde*
*il giovane cuore di mia madre avvolto intorno a me*
*mia sorella che piangeva per pane e mortadella.*
*ancora due notti*
*in un treno rigido e freddo*
*verso Toronto*
*dove le braccia aperte*
*di un uomo mezzo dimenticato*
*aspettavano*

## RETURNING

we don't discuss the distance anymore
returning is now
the other dream
not American at all
not Canadian or Italian
it has lost its nationality.
in the sixties we came in swarms like summer bees
smelling of something strange
wearing the last moist kiss
of our own sky.
we came with heavy trunks
empty pockets
and a dream.

I was one of them
tucked away below the sea line
on the bottom floor of a ship
that swelled and ached
for thirteen days
our bellies emptied into the Atlantic
until the ship finally vomited
on the shores of Halifax
there, where the arms and legs
of my doll fell apart into the sea
finding their way back over the waves.

my mother's young heart wrapped around me
my sister crying for bread and *mortadella*.
we held on
two more nights on a stiff, cold train
headed for Toronto
where the open arms of a half forgotten man
waited.

**Why did you choose this book for translation?**

Because it was the first one, the first book was such an important achievement for me, when finally somebody actually said: "Yes we want to publish your words, in English." I thought then that the first book needed to have a life in Italian also. If there is any interest in this one, the rest will follow. And also because it represented so much of the angst of the young woman who came to this country, and had to survive it and find her place in it. It was the beginning of the struggle of the dreams, the fear, alienation, the relationships, rejections, the search for identity; it is all in that first book, the pain, the love. Not that the others don't address many of the same themes, they do, but when you're starting your journey as a young woman, you remember the first love, the first kiss with such intensity.

DONNE ITALIANE

> *Senti le nostre donne*
> *Il silenzio che fanno.*
> (Rocco Scotellaro)

ecco le donne
nate per dare vita
respirano solo
aria avanzata
e parlano solo
quando voci più dure
si sono addormentate

le ho viste sanguinare
nel buio
nascondendo dentro
le macchie
come peccati
chiedendo scusa

le ho viste avvolgere l'anima

intorno ai figli
e servire il loro cuore
in un pranzo che non
condividono mai.

## ITALIAN WOMEN

these are the women
who were born to give birth
they breathe only
leftover air
and speak only
when deeper voices
have fallen asleep
I have seen them bleed
in the dark
hiding the stains inside them
like sins
apologizing
I have seen them wrap their souls
around their children
and serve their own hearts
in a meal they never
share.

**Bearing in mind the theme of the Atri conference (return journey, or reverse journeys), in what way was the act of translating or participating in the translation of Italian Women and Other Tragedies a journey of return?**

That's a difficult question. Going back to Italy, over the years, I always felt as if Italy had, in some way, gotten rid of me. It had disposed of me, let me go; *ciao baby, you don't belong here anymore*, and every time I returned I expected to be embraced, welcomed but it seemed we "immigrants" were largely forgotten and no one was really interested in our stories.

It was important for me to have a book in my "native language," not to justify... *demand*... that they recognize I was part of that country – part of that language – part of that culture. It was, in a strange way, my passport back, because I don't have an Italian passport that says I was a citizen of this land.

What would you call that? [Gianna is still seeking the right word...] A *validation* that I belonged somewhere, that I originally began somewhere. I wanted to bring a little bit back to that place. It was important for me, that I wasn't totally rejected, a misplaced shoe – thrown away. Somehow that misplaced shoe wanted to find its way back, to leave a print.

Acceptance may be an illusion – they may reject you anyway, even if you go back with an Italian book – but they can't deny the fact that it exists – hate me, reject me, but I'm here, I have the passport to prove it, ha.

**Were there surprises, in this translation?**

No, no big surprises, just hard work, focus, there were moments that made me feel closer to the memory of the initial inspiration of the poem. The language takes you back to a particular moment and time. An example: "My mother tells me stories."

*Mamma mi racconta storie* – Mom and me walking the streets of my hometown, skipping the cobblestones, eating ice cream. In Italian, as I read it, it made me feel almost as if I was in that piazza again, walking over those cobblestones, wanting ice cream. The language made me feel the experience in the way it had been lived – originally.

But Italian is not my language anymore, my dialect is more representative of me because I still speak the dialect with my 86-year-old mother and have always spoken it with her and my aunts.

My poems are much more important to me, in English, than they are in Italian. But it's not to say that I don't appreciate and enjoy them in Italian. It goes back to the idea that they weren't born in that language but found home in it anyway, the way I found home in Canada.

### MAMMA MI RACCONTA STORIE

mamma mi racconta storie
dei miei vestiti di cotone bianco
dei miei lunghi boccoli neri
I giorni a Ceprano
le tenevo la mano e saltellavo
su tutte le selci
di via Alfieri
mia sorella voleva sempre il gelato
"ti ricordi?" mi chiede
le sue dita ancora imboccolano I miei capelli
voglio urlare

"no!"
mi stringe al suo petto
un tempo
vicino a un camino
non dormivo se non ero
al suo petto
i suoi occhi
sempre umidi
mentre mi chiama ancora
bimba


## MOTHER TELLS ME STORIES

mother tells me stories
of my white cotton dresses
and my long black curls
the days in Ceprano
i held her hand and skipped
all the cobblestones in
via Alfieri
my sister always wanted ice cream
'do you remember?' she asks
her fingers making ringlets in my hair
i want to scream 'I don't!'
she holds me to her breast
there was a time
by a fireplace
i would not fall asleep
but at her breast
her eyes
are always wet
as she calls me
*bimba*

## About "'Sta Vita":

This poem, written in my dialect, the dialect that I speak and remember, I tried to translate into English, but I don't think it works well in English because it was truly a piece born in dialect. It's not in the original book published in English. I added it to this translation, almost as a little gift to my mother, to my town. In English, it sounds rather juvenile, or sentimental. In its dialect, it has emotion, strength, power; it has a definite sense of loss and melancholy, the language gives it that intensity.

**I ask Gianna for the gist of it, in English, because although I have heard her read this poem several times to live audiences, I do not have sufficient command of Italian to comprehend it. On the spot, Gianna gave me the gist, thus:**

THIS LIFE

who would have ever thought of it.
this life.
so many steps I have taken,
so many days that have gone by,
so many tears and sacrifices.
and at the end,
what will I leave you,
my daughter.
a little house?
small, but paid for.
that gold medal your father gave me,
they stole from me.
no money. no gold.
my daughter, so many things that I would leave you,
but all that remains, is this dialect,
this dialect that you don't quite understand.
it's a gift without a price.
a sort of poem.
but when we are together, silent, very silent
and calm
listen, listen,
my daughter.
how loud this heart beats.

So, the translation gives you the sense of the poem, but it's the words in dialect that give you the music and the power, and *that* was born in the dialect. I love the dialect. Really, the first language is the dialect. Italian is the second. English is the third. The third has become the first. The second is the second. And the first is the third. Isn't it interesting, the way everything gets turned around?

*Gianna refers to the quote at the front of the book:* "Every language I speak is a second language" *because, really, language… but she never completes her thought, gets lost in contemplation.*

'STA VITA

   chi se le fusse mai credute
   'sta vita
   quanta passe
   che sso ffatte
   quanta ggiorne
   sen'aue ite
   quanta piante
   e sacrifice
   e alla fine
   che te lasse
   figlia mia
   che te lasse....
   na casa
   piccula
   ma pagata
   chella medaglia d'oro
   che padrte me dette
   me l'au rubata
   niente soldi e nient'oro
   figlia mia
   quante cose
   i te desse
   ma sule ste dialette me rimane
   ste dialette che quase quase
   n'capisce
   e' ne regale senza prezze
   na specie de poesia
   e quande stame 'nzieme
   zitte, zitte
   calme, calme
   siente, siente
   bella figlia mia
   come ste core
   forte
   bbatte.

**I ask Gianna to tell me about the actual journey of return – to promote the book:**

I went to two universities – to Bologna, and the University of Naples, Orientale. They were having conferences there, and they invited me to present my work. I was a little reluctant, because it was at a university level, full of academics and students, and I knew I was coming with a book that was very personal, and a language that was very personal, and perhaps not the academic Italian that they may have been looking for, so I was a little bit frightened, but I was totally wrong, because they embraced the work, so well. And I think it was because they understood where the work was coming from, a place of sincerity and honesty and experience. It was not making any pretensions about being more than what it was – the voice of a woman and her experiences, her view of life, love, death and in that voice they found something they could relate to, something that touches all human experience.

I had some academics in tears, a lot of them, that was interesting, and the students were very receptive. They all wanted books, asked questions about the history of immigration I had lived. I think the political reality of Italy today has brought many students to finally look at what happened to those of us who left in great numbers and made our lives in foreign places. Today Italy is facing many challenges (with their new arrivals), the same challenges we found as immigrants to other places. But I was happy to find that there was a real embracing and a curiosity – not only of my work, but also of me as a woman, a person, a writer, an ex-Italian living in Canada. I was surprised and very honoured by that. I thought it would have been different. Italians in today's Italy present an arrogance at times, a sense of, let's call it *style,* that doesn't always make one comfortable. The immigrant experience is not exactly at the top of their list in terms of interest or appreciation. Let's face it – they have looked down on us a little bit, maybe a little embarrassed by us, the uneducated, poor, rural *contadini* that left in shiploads. I did think they were going to be critical and perhaps dismissive, but I was wrong, at least in the experience I had at the two universities, I didn't find that. The students were lovely. They were curious. They were interested. They were appreciative. The academics – the same.

But it was fucking cold. It was the most unusual October they'd ever had. I was in Bologna, October 15, and Naples, October 19. I bought a winter coat in Bologna that cleaned out my wallet. I couldn't get warm. It was humid, windy, and rainy. I kept dreaming of my Canadian furnace deep in the heart of my basement. I wanted to go home to the furnace. In the hotels I was o.k., but when I stayed with my cousins – they still have fireplaces, some have electrical heating but they are careful in using it, electricity is so expensive in Italy they don't always switch it on when they should. All those homes with stone walls and marble floors. I went to church one Sunday all bundled and cloaked with hat and gloves and looking around that magnificent structure with stained glass windows and flickering wax candles I swear I saw the statues shivering from the cold.

One of my friends asked me, did you bring the wool *"cannottiera"*? Wool camisole. It has to be wool to absorb the humidity. He told me I'd better go to the market on Saturday and buy a couple of dozen. Isn't it ironic: wanting to come home to Canada – to get warm? Wasn't I supposed to be in sunny Italy????? Not in October.

# Nino Ricci's Mythopoiesis: Where Has <u>He</u> Gone?

*Maria Giuseppina Cesari*

THE HEADING "NINO RICCI'S MYTHOPOIESIS: Where Has <u>He</u> Gone?" is a clear allusion to Ricci's book title *Where <u>She</u> Has Gone* as well as a question on the novelist's authorial and critical position. *Where <u>She</u> Has Gone* is the third novel of Ricci's *Trilogy* about Italian immigration, the previous two being the acclaimed *Lives of the Saints* and *In a Glass House*. Many critics consider *Lives of the Saints* and *Where <u>She</u> Has Gone* novels with an Italian flavour, as opposed to *In a Glass House*, a novel with an Italian Canadian ambiance. However, between the two Italian-based novels, *Where She Has Gone* often ranks second after the most celebrated *Lives of the Saints*. Although it is less well-known, *Where She Has Gone* is central to the concept of homecoming for three reasons. First of all, the main character, Viktor/Vittorio goes back to his native village in Valle del Sole (Sun Valley) in Molise after twenty years in Toronto. Then the novel ends the epic of the Innocente family and the entire *Trilogy*. Finally, the book shows a mythical Italy where Viktor tries to reconstruct his family history and his Italian roots. The geography of the author's mind permeates real descriptions and facts: consequently, although Ricci is likely to recall some family experiences and historical data of his *Molise*, he paints an imaginary homeland of ancient traditions and cruel fate.

My paper interrogates whether an immigrant like Viktor may succeed in going back home to Italy and whether this journey back may be a catharsis for the main character and the author himself. The "she" in the *Where She Has Gone* title refers to Rita, Vittorio Innocente's stepsister, who goes back to Europe flying from Ontario and her incestuous love with her half brother Viktor. However, she is manifestly Vittorio's double and he cannot but follow her to Italy and to England. Viktor/Vittorio's journey traces her steps back to Italy. His trip becomes for him an interior journey back to his roots and the land of his ancestors.

In *Where She Has Gone*, Viktor's going back to Italy can be interpreted by reading myth as its central focus. The Italian Canadian Viktor goes back to a mythic Italy where every detail stays fixed in a timeless space. When Viktor tries to compare memory with actual facts, they clash. Like his own memory, his mother's remembrance fades away. Viktor finds an old picture showing him and his mother Cristina the day of their departure. His mother has "such a look of the mountain peasant" (*Where* 190) and she does not look like the fighter who has defied society and customs in *Lives of the Saints*.

Ricci reads myth in its wider meaning, as an archetype of the human condition, as a symbolic interpretation and as a narrative device. As an "archetype" he applies Joseph Campbell's framework of the monomyth to Viktor's journey: although the hero is forced to cross the ocean, he does not choose to go. He looks for the magic gift (boon), but he has not found it in Canada so far. He finally goes back to Italy looking for it in the third book of the *Trilogy*. However, Viktor's journey back to Italy to find his way home does not lead to a definite solution. Italy represents his roots, his heritage but there is no catharsis, no salvation at the end of the *Trilogy*. Viktor admits:

> My second departure from Valle del Sole, twenty years after the first, becomes more final and more fatal. (*Where* 302)

In Ricci's "going back" novel, the mythical image of an ancient Italy, full of ruins and magic stories, goes hand in hand with other myths. First of all, the writer expands on the myth of Oedipus, i.e. Viktor's love for his unconventional mother (*Lives of the Saints*), with the myth of incest, the forbidden love for his stepsister Rita. The case of incest with Viktor's stepsister is another example of how the writer uses myth as an archetype and a symbolic interpretation. Incest is part of the universal myth of Oedipus, and it also recalls Aristophanes' myth of the two halves in Plato's *Symposium*.[1] The original division of human beings in two halves and their subsequent quest to be reunited in love are clearly explained by Rita. When Viktor is not there, she misses him in a "crazy" way, she feels that he is part of her own body. Rita says:

> [...] it's like you were inside me somehow, like you were a lung or a heart, something I couldn't do without. I never thought it was love or anything like that. It was more – crazy than that. Like not knowing where my own body ended. Just crazy (*Where* 256).

When Viktor and Rita cannot be reunited, Viktor loses the other half of his own self. He attempts suicide and then he flies to a far away island, off the Kenyan coast. There he finally starts writing his own story. In conclusion, going back to Italy is not a final catharsis for Viktor. The journey back treats his inner wounds but it does not completely heal them. In order to be healed he has to write his way out of distress and displacement. As a narrative device, Plato's myth is replaced by the myth of journey or *nostos*[2] and by the artist's trust in his own creation. Like Ulysses, Viktor is forever journeying and forever searching but there is hope at the end of the tunnel when he states: "The *path I was on was neither gentle nor steep [...]*."(*Where* 321)

If there is no final catharsis in "going back to Italy" and creative writing is the ultimate answer for the main character of the novel, can the author appease his soul and his past? Also, can Ricci reconcile his ethnic and global identity by creative writing? In fact, the other allusion in my title "Where Has He Gone?" refers to my meeting with Ricci at the Leacock Summer Festival in July 2009. He was introduced as a Canadian writer of Italian descent. Instead, when I directly asked him how he wanted to be defined, he answered: "As a global writer." His answer brings me back to the question "Where has he gone?" As I am persuaded that he can be both an ethnic writer and a global writer, I would like to suggest that he must have found a coherent and comprehensive theoretical framework to keep the two sides of his ethnic and global identity together.

This coherent and comprehensive theoretical framework is represented by myth. In many interviews Ricci explained how Italian culture had been a burden to him, almost a frightening heritage. He often felt that it did not belong to him completely.[3] Nevertheless, in his youth he spent a year studying in Florence and trying to come to terms with his Italian roots. Like his double Viktor, Ricci travelled to Nigeria and worked there as an English teacher. The myth of journey and the myth of salvation through artistic imagination are relevant for the character, for the writer and for the man. Besides, myth remains a threading line in his more recent works. In his novel

*Testament*, Ricci moves on to the universal myth of Jesus, then in *The Origin of Species* he deals with the myth of Darwin. In his *Pierre Elliott Trudeau* biography he describes the P.M. as a mythic figure. In the novel *The Origin of Species* the two final myths of *Where She Has Gone*, the journey and the creative imagination, appear again together. In this novel he deals with evolutionary theory and its influence on narrative structures. There is another initiation journey too, this time to the Galapagos Islands, where Alex, the main character, has a revelation.

Myth is central to all his works and it represents his solution to be global and stay ethnic. Ricci is global when he confronts himself with universal figures like Jesus, Darwin, and Canadian relevant figures, like Pierre Elliott Trudeau, or when he writes about universal myths. The myth of journey, the myth of Oedipus, the myth of ancient Italy, the myth of creative imagination are all part of his world vision. They have all been explored since his early works. As a consequence, there is not such a division between his *Trilogy* about the immigrant experience and his later works about global figures, the former being regarded as "ethnic" and the latter as "universal." Ricci has shifted from being Italian Canadian to being Canadian Italian or – as he prefers it – being a global writer of Italian descent.

Yet, the ethnic writer is still there in the background. In *The Origin of Species* the main character's name is Alex Fratarcangeli. He is an Italian Canadian PhD student living in Montreal and he has an Italian last name. Fratarcangeli is an ironic reference to religious matters, "frate" meaning friar and "arcangeli" meaning "archangels." He comes from Ontario, like Ricci himself, and he has a mother with an "italianese"[4] vocabulary. Even in his latest work, the Pierre Elliott Trudeau biography,[5] when he speaks of the mythical images of his youth, he remembers the pictures of John F. Kennedy and Pope John XXIII on his mother's kitchen wall. President Kennedy is the real American myth and Pope John XXIII is the real Catholic myth.

References to his and his family's Italian Canadian roots are still present. If Ricci does not write about immigration anymore, his form, his content, his references are still ethnic and above all his thought is still ethnic. He has shifted from writing about the immigrant experience to writing from the point of view of the immigrant experience. In conclusion, he is still "going back" to Italy, but in a different way. From this perspective he is a forerunner. Maybe this is the reason why President Barrack Obama was supposedly reading Ricci's *The Origin of Species*.[6]

## Notes

1. Plato, *Symposium*. During the Symposium, Aristophanes gives his opinion about love and tells the story of the myth of the two halves. Once men were perfect and they had everything. There was no difference between men and women, but Zeus, who was jealous of such perfection, divided them in two halves. Since then each of us is constantly looking for his/her half, because when the other half is reunited, everybody recovers his/her lost perfection. Il mito delle due metà: "Ciascuno pensa semplicemente che il dio ha espresso ciò che da lungo tempo senza dubbio desiderava: riunirsi e fondersi con l'altra anima. Non più due, ma un'anima sola." Available at <Http://www.girodivite.it/Il-mito-delle-due-metadiPlatone.html>

2. On this aspect see all classical and literary references like Homer's *Odyssey* and Joyce's *Ulysses*. In ancient Greece the word *nostos* refers both to the journey back home of Greek heroes from Troy and to the story of this journey.

3. Nino Ricci: "I'd been to my mother's village, which Valle del Sole is based on." See also Mary Rimmer's interview with Nino Ricci: "Nino Ricci: A Big Canvas" in *Studies in Canadian Literature*, Fredericton, CA: University of New Brunswick, Vol.18.02 1993: available at <http://www.lib.unb.ca/Texts/SCL/>

4. For the definition of "Italianese" literature see Filippo Salvatore's works, for example *Ancient Memories, Modern Identities* (translated by Domenic Cusmano), Montréal: Guernica Editions, 1999.

5. Nino Ricci, *Pierre Elliott Trudeau*. Extraordinary Canadians Coll., Toronto: Penguin Canada, 2009.

6. Reference available at Nino Ricci's own website: http://ninoricci.com/news/barack-obama-to-visit-ricci-web-site

## Works Cited

Alfano, Michele. "Saints and the Hereafter: an Interview with Nino Ricci" in *VIA*, Vol. 6, n. 2: 11-31.

Campbell, Joseph. *The Hero with a Thousand Faces*. Princeton, USA: Princeton U.P. (1949) 1973.

_____. (Italian translation) *L'eroe dai mille volti*. Parma: Guanda, 2000.

Cesari, Maria Giuseppina. Personal Conversation with Nino Ricci. Leacock Summer Festival, Ontario, July 2009.

De Franceschi, Marisa. "A Theory of Everything" in *ACCENTI*, n. 15, Montréal: Winter 2009: 34.

Di Michele, Mary. "Un piccolo rinascimento" in *Writers in Transition, The Proceedings of the First National Conference of Italian-Canadian Writers*, ed. by C. Dino Minni and Anna Foschi Ciampolini, Toronto: Guernica Editions, 1990: 16-17.

Frye, Northrop. *Anatomy of Criticism. Four Essays*. Princeton, USA: Princeton U.P., 1957.

_____. *Anatomia della critica. Quattro saggi.* Italian translation by Paola Rosa-Clot and Sandro Stratta, 2nd. ed. Torino: Einaudi, 1969.

Gorlier, Claudio. "La letteratura nella seconda lingua della diaspora" in *Itinera*, ed. by Maddalena Tirabassi, Torino: ed. Fondazione Giovanni Agnelli, 2005:173-183.

Guzzo McParland, Connie. "Nino Ricci. Getting to the origin of things" in *PanoramItalia*, Vol. 4 n. 2, Montréal: Summer 2009: 27.

Ricci, Nino. *Lives of the Saints.* Dunvegan: Cormorant Books, 1990.

_____. *In A Glass House.* Toronto: McClelland & Stewart, 1993.

_____. *Where She Has Gone.* Toronto: McClelland & Stewart, 1997.

_____. *Testament.* Toronto: Anchor Canada, 2002.

_____. *The Origin of Species.* Toronto: Anchor Canada, 2008.

_____. *Pierre Elliott Trudeau.* Extraordinary Canadians Coll., Toronto: Penguin Canada, 2009.

# Sweet Lemons 2: Discovery and Memory[1]

### Delia De Santis & Venera Fazio

AFTER CO-EDITOR VENERA FAZIO AND I assembled all the manuscripts for the multi-genre anthology *Sweet Lemons 2*, we realized that our goals for the content of the book had shifted. We were not the ones who had brought about the change, but it was the writing of our contributors that had changed. Their main focus was no longer the same as for *Sweet Lemons*, volume one, the purpose of which had been to celebrate Sicilian immigrants and to explore the diverse way in which Sicilian heritage manifests itself after generations of immigration. The contributors had now moved on from stories of immigration to stories of mainly discovery and memory: recalling, remembering, and trying to hang on to a heritage that now seemed more and more distant. They were searching and trying to recapture how it used to be, simultaneously conceding that a great part of their legacy had vanished in the years that passed after the migration of their ancestors to their new world.

For example, in the short story "The Sleeping Stranger" by Sicilian Australian writer Venero Armanno, the widow Grace goes back to calling herself Graziella now that she is old; a small gesture with significant symbolism, as if she is trying to recapture all that she has lost. Armanno explains: "In those young days they called her Grace because Graziella came off their tongues like ash and iron filings, so now when she found the stranger curled up and sleeping with her dogs, the first thing she wondered was what his name was, and how it might sound in his new country" (227).

In this poignant story, as Graziella is dying and *lo straniero* is about to be caught, with the certainty that he will be shot by those who are hunting him, Graziella finally sees clearly "what had led to it; to come to the stranger carrying a shotgun. To let suspicion take root and grow. Her father, [...] he wouldn't have done it this way. His hand would have come out first, in friendship" (237).

She doesn't feel a strong pull for the country of her ancestors, but she is mourning the loss of the values of her Sicilian father as well as her failure to pass some of these same values on to her son, Joe, and his brothers. "For a moment Graziella even contemplated the impossible –talking Joe into actively helping – but the timbre of his voice and the quality of his hostility stayed with her (233)" so she remained silent. "The bastards know they got no chance," Joe said to her. "You make sure you keep the bloody shotgun handy, all right? I checked it for you" (233).

From North America, New York writer and poet Nick Matros contributed a poem titled "Sicily, Am I Still Sicilian to You?". In the poem he asks:

> But am I still Sicilian if I don't
> Tattoo on a tightly wound tricep
> The *tri-colore* in the shape of the sacred island
> If I don't wear my gold cross
> And hang a dying Christ over my bed
> And be sure to get racist
> And stubborn anytime anyone mentions
> Moorish roots? (345)

Are there answers to Matros' questions? This, in itself, is another question. In any case, these questions inspire a certain longing to discover more about one's heritage and a need to retrieve images from one's past – which, at times, can be a frenzied search, a chase for something elusive, something that is quickly slipping away.

Jim Pignetti, a writer from the US, strongly feels the loss of that "other" language or culture. He expresses this loss in a poem in which the form itself makes the words rebound on the page, much like the sound of the Sicilian words still trapped in his head. But that's all that remains. Nevertheless, those sounds are still with him, strong, sharp, and perhaps not as much a lost world as he believes it to be:

### Lost World

>     watching  *lassa mi stari*  hearing
> the words bounce   maronna
>       along the ceiling  brutta, figliu   they gather
>           picciuteddru, beddra, mortu
>   miserabili
>              swirling
> bathing the boy   iddru, dura, friddu   in a language
>       he'll never have. ( 343)

Frank Polizzi, editor of the literary journal *Feile-Festa*, in his memorable poem "Zampogna," talks about first losing his family's language, "then its culture / and even the extended clan / somewhere in the center of America" (353). Despite the fact that not all of his losses can be regained, he makes a strong, spirited attempt to recapture sounds that were familiar to his ancestors after finding a zampogna in a dark cellar. The name *Zampogna* is stitched on the dusty cover of the instrument. He carries it upstairs, in his arms, protectively – to the light, where he can better examine it. He then loses little time researching the strange instrument, and discovers it is "some distant Celtic cousin to the bagpipe!" (354), and that it is actually called *cornamusa* in Sicilian. His research prompts him to experience digitally the "mystifying melodies" from *Bagpipes of the World* from an old PC.

Of the *cornamusa*, Polizzi poeticizes:

> I imagined that its notes must have cascaded
> down those island-mountain slopes,
> melancholy music for *i poveri*,
> filling in the cracks of homes,
> scored in surrounding stone
> and lost *in tempo* over generations. (354)

Melancholy is the term that best describes the state of once belonging to another culture: the blood of one's ancestors in one's veins, but possessing only faint or fleeting memories of their faces, if any at all. Yet so much lingers, as seen in the above stanza of Polizzi's poem, where through ancient music, the poet, although mystified, reconnects with the soul of his *antenati*:

> To be honest, I had trouble fathoming the music,
> yet the sound coyly echoed in my thoughts
> that swept all the way
> to the island of sun and winds. (355)

The poem ends with: "This was a time to listen, / a time to reflect, / *chi sacciu*, maybe a time to travel / to the deepest pitches of its call / in the heat of summer." (355)

Cristina Trapani-Scott, a Sicilian-American, born and raised in Detroit, Michigan, wrote a poem entitled "A Photo on the Cellar Wall." This touching poem takes us from the new world back to the old world:

> Sicily must be another world to my
> father who grew up in Detroit.
> I've seen the all-American photo
> of him as a boy [...]
> [...] where he's posed
> in a white baseball uniform
> ready to take a swing.
>
> Another picture, maybe a similar one,
> hung once on a cellar wall in Trapani.
> [...]
>
> My mother told me [...]
> that my father's grandfather kept the picture
> on the cellar wall to kiss when he went to retrieve wine
> for dinner. I pictured him descending
> into the dark cellar, one hand fishing
> for the pull switch, the other
> brushing the wall searching for the photo,
> pausing to feel something beyond
> the smooth finish,
> to see color in black and white memory. (341-342)
> [...]

Trapani-Scott has recreated her own tender memory, from something her mother had told her from the past. In her imagined world she tries "to feel something beyond / the smooth finish" by reaching back in time, peeling away layers of lost memory.

In a prose poem titled "*Sita 'mmaculata* – Immaculate Silk" by Canadian writer Bruna Di Giuseppe-Bertoni, the widow Nicolina, a member of Bertoni's seniors' group, tells of when she was a young girl back in Sicily. Eyes watering, Nicolina recalls of the courage it took to escape the fate of an arranged marriage. She wistfully mourns having to leave her beautiful wedding dress behind. "Pearls adorned the neckline," she says, "*di sita 'mmaculata era*" (332). Nicolina was only fifteen and her mother wanted her to marry a cousin twelve years her senior. However, her destiny changed when she met a young man from America who had come home to find a bride. They fell for each other, and her aunt helped her to escape, avoiding bloodshed:

> 'He'd be killed if word got out about our plan.
> I left home like a ghost in the middle of the night
> and met the stranger by a roadside.
> *Nu mi scantaiu*,' Nicolina said with certainty.
> 'I knew he would be a good husband
> My wedding dress was left hanging in the closet.
> The journey to America was my honeymoon.' (333)

Even though Nicolina has had a good life in the new country, her story is one of loss. "Her eyes water," as she speaks of the beautiful wedding dress she never got to wear, and has never forgotten. All the dreams of a young girl had to be left behind forever, like her dress, "hanging in a closet." Even without regrets, having to leave home and country, "like a ghost in the middle of the night," was not an easy price for Nicolina to pay.

Louisa Calio, poet, writer, and performer, speaks to the Sicilian's sense of belonging, in her poem "Cells Remember the Dark Mother":

> Sicily my dark mother
> and other island of light
> mighty land of contradictions, complications
> multiplicities and many crossroads.
> At last I've come to comprehend
> my sense of belonging to all those other peoples. (364)

We hope that the writing of this new anthology will be fruitful in rekindling a desire for a greater depth in the search of one's roots. A search that would take us back to the sounds of *cornamusa* over the hills of that triangular island in the Mediterranean, to stepping carefully back into the dark cellars of our ancestors, searching for "the faces on the walls." This endeavour would undoubtedly give rise to a world of torn bits and pieces of remembrances, little threads that can be pulled to open up small vistas into the chambers of the forgotten, creating a greater yearning for what could soon be lost forever.

Following the publishing of *Sweet Lemons 2*, where will the writing for the third volume take us? For a moment, I will take us back to Louisa Calio, who may provide the answer in the poem "Signifying Woman – An Italian American Jazz Poem" when she says:

Sicilian queen,
a dew's drop on mint green
Pure, liquid, mercury,
a grain of sand in the Sahara
& between cracks of concrete.
She is the wave length Green
fish-bellied, crab-crawling, moon-child,
secret reptile, Virgin &
Mean ...
the final curtain
called
before the Great Silencing. (362-363)

Yet, it is hard to imagine a "great silencing," a closed book on Sicilian culture for people of Sicilian origin, whose forefathers and foremothers migrated away from their homeland in search of a better life for themselves and their children.

## Note

1. All texts cited are published in *Sweet Lemons 2*. Eds. Venera Fazio and Delia De Santis. Mineola, NY & Ottawa: Legas 2010.

# Tra Scozia e Italia: identità, differenza e poetica interculturale in William Sharp

*Annalisa Bonomo*

F U L'IDEA DI UNA POETICA volutamente interculturale a costituire le fondamenta della letteratura del poeta scozzese William Sharp.

Viaggiatore alla scoperta di sempre nuove terre d'approdo, geografiche e spirituali al contempo, Sharp incarnò l'essenza stessa di un'esistenza personale e artistica a cavallo tra terre e lingue spesso in conflitto tra loro, distanti per matrice ed impatto culturale. Scozzese di nascita ma cosmopolita nell'animo e spesso restio alle rigidità dello spirito nazionalista tipico del vittorianesimo di fine '800, Sharp costituì un mirabile esempio di critico acuto e scrittore attento, poeta raffinato e biografo esperto, viaggiatore in piena sintonia con il mondo terrestre e dunque artista moderno ed eclettico in ogni sua manifestazione.

Già nel 1911 Richard Le Gallienne s'interrogava su quello che egli stesso definiva *a certain histrionism* di Sharp, puntando l'attenzione sulla criptica rappresentazione dei suoi "sé" sfociata nel perpetuo incontro/scontro con l'affascinante e controverso *alter-ego* femminile, Fiona Macleod, nei cui panni firmò i suoi scritti migliori consacrandosi alla critica come "poet-essa" sopraffina. Lo sviluppo di una doppia personalità, custodita segretamente e protetta sino al giorno della sua scomparsa avvenuta nel 1905, insieme all'espansione verso una sensibilità poetica dai caratteri marcatamente femminili, fecero di Macleod una delle più autorevoli voci della *Celtic Twilight School*; tradussero un "neo-romanticismo" dai colori accesi del *pastiche* e della *vagueness*, incarnando il fascino (tipico del suo tempo) per il "diverso", lo "straniero" e il "misterioso" – a volte ossessivamente rappresentato da un mitico e archetipico *taste for places*, manifestazione di un'ottica plurale che accompagnò Sharp/Macleod lungo le molteplici fasi della propria produzione letteraria. Come affermava Flavia Alaya nell'ormai lontano 1970 in *William Sharp – "Fiona Macleod"*:

> He was in flight – in flight from the orthodoxies and convictions that a century of political expansion had given to the individual Englishman to secure his identity with the National fate and turn the romantic's sense of dislocation, and in quest for identity, to excellent political use. (Alaya 1970: 13)

Alla luce di simili considerazioni, i suoi frenetici e continui viaggi ci restituiscono il quadro di una personalità poetica all'insegna di una difficile identificazione. Ne rimane piena testimonianza nell'intenso *William Sharp, Fiona Macleod: A Memoir*, a firma della compagna di sempre, Elizabeth Sharp, la quale, nella sezione "First Visit to America" scrive: "Born, as he would say, with the wandering wave in his blood, the fixed and the inevitable, were antipathetic to him." (*A Memoir* I, 238)

La poetica di Sharp, infatti, parte dalla Scozia e attraversa l'Australia; riparte dai mari del Sud per ritornare a Londra; riscopre la Francia, la Germania e l'America; affonda in Africa per riemergere nell'antica Grecia e morire in Italia; accompagna, in altre parole, l'artista e l'uomo attraverso le diverse fasi di una *quest* perpetua, lungo una ricerca di una rotta e di un approdo che avessero il sapore di un definitivo "ritorno a casa."

Una simile e smaniosa ricerca dai caratteri inter/intraculturali guidò Sharp in Italia: quest'ultima, rimase la controparte più amata della Scozia natale, una "nuova casa" presso cui riposare: "For the first time have seen the Sicilian Highlands with the beauty of Scotland" (*A Memoir* II: 322); il paesaggio e i profumi della Sicilia (in cui il poeta morì), tradussero, infatti, una definitiva empatia romantica con i luoghi. Alla maniera di una nuova *divine adventure* (titolo di una delle sue raccolte più rappresentative del 1900) vissuta alle pendici dell'Etna tra il profumo inebriante dei pistacchi della città di Bronte e nello splendido scenario offerto dal castello della Ducea dei Nelson (in località di Maniace, ove tuttora il poeta riposa), Sharp diede libero sfogo alla sua anima romantica e vagabonda, abbracciando per l'ultima volta il mondo con animo illusionista:

> He did not see places or men and women as they were! He did not care to see them so: but he had quite peculiar powers of assimilating to himself foreign associations – the ideas, the colours, the current allusions, of foreign worlds. In Italy he became an Italian in spirit; in Algiers, an Arab. (*A Memoir* I: 170)

Negli ultimi tempi trascorsi in Sicilia e in entrambe le *personae* di Sharp, macrocosmo e microcosmo magicamente coincisero, rintracciando nel linguaggio della natura il definitivo incanto. D'altra parte, il senso di ogni singola scoperta partecipava al tentativo di ricostruire una sistematica identità nazionale che condividesse, in veste del tutto rinnovata, caratteri universali da un lato e nazionalistici dall'altro, costituendo, dunque, una risposta alla storia letteraria e culturale del suo tempo. Scriveva infatti Alaya:

> It was Mme de Staël who had led the English to discover, with such delight and awe, their own National character, and it was through her, certainly, that cultural determinism was assisted in its way to England and influenced the thinking of the English on issues of nationalism. That famous Victorian byproduct, the fascination with Italy (eventually to play so important a part in Sharp's career), was a result of this influence combined with the sense of place already described: it was a country where characteristic and compelling places had proliferated in semi-tropical abundance; and it was also a symbol of the national character discovering its homeland, its physical definition. (Alaya: 14)

L'eterogeneità dei suoi scritti unitamente alla criptica rappresentazione dei suoi sé (che non furono solo due ma tre, compreso *Wilfion*, con cui Elisabeth Sharp identificò il completamento tra le due prospettive originarie) condussero Sharp stesso a confessare e motivare le dinamiche della sua "creazione." Si veda qui di seguito un estratto da una lettera a Mrs Janvier:

> This rapt sense of oneness with nature, this cosmic ecstasy and elation, this wayfaring along the extreme verges of the common world, all this is so wrought up with the romance of life that I could not bring myself to expression by my outer self insistent and tyrannical as that need is. My truest self, the self who is below all other selves and my most intimate life and joys and suffering, thoughts, emotions and dreams must find expression. (*A Memoir* II, 227)

I ripetuti spostamenti divennero testimonianza di un raffinato atteggiamento romantico della fuga, della ricerca dell'altro da sé, della volontà di fagocitare il mondo insieme alle sensazioni fisiche e spirituali che ne costituiscono l'essenza, il tutto indirizzato verso la riscrittura di una via del ritorno, fatta spesso coincidere con i luoghi più intimi dell'anima piuttosto che con un unico spazio geografico di riferimento.

Pellegrino dell'essere, la natura rappresentò per Sharp la principale fonte d'ispirazione: egli stesso affermava: "but my heart is a lonely hunter that hunts on a lonely hill" (Macleod, 1914:27); cacciatore su una collina, dunque, una collina che potremmo dire grande quanto tutto il mondo, quello interno ed esterno di un artista capace di caricare ogni luogo di una personalità e di un carattere individuale e universale al contempo; una collina sulla quale il mondo naturale e quello degli uomini si muovono in maniera simbiotica e corrispondente.

L'energia di alcuni tra i suoi più alti momenti poetici non riesce comunque a colmare quel vuoto persistente e drammatico che ricoprì tutta la sua produzione. La ricerca di un'appartenenza perduta, i tentativi di ricomporre un itinerario intimo e privato rimasero, infatti, incompiuti – almeno all'interno del modo fisico e terrestre; la definitiva identificazione con una nuova comunità, la conclusione consapevole di un viaggio nella propria identità, insieme al ritrovamento di un unico luogo in cui fermarsi per sempre e riposare, sembravano essergli preclusi dalla sua stessa natura. Si legge in una sua lettera del 7 marzo 1902: "My wife says I am never satisfied, and that Paradise itself would be intolerable for me if I could not get out of it when I wanted." (*A Memoir* II : 340) Ogni viaggio aveva dunque lo scopo di ricomporre un quadro più ampio, un'esperienza dei luoghi che avesse un valore etico, morale e simbolico non necessariamente delimitata da ristretti confini geografici.

Ed è rileggendo *By Sundown Shores* (raccolta a firma di Fiona Macleod del 1900, pubblicata a cura di Thomas B. Mosher nel 1902) che si palesa una simile rivelazione. A tracciare il filo conduttore della preziosa raccolta – pare ve ne siano solo circa 400 copie – v'è l'unicità delle leggende e dei miti, identici in Scozia come in Siria e in tutto il mondo; v'è l'universalità del loro valore nella storia degli uomini.

Anche in questo caso, la riscoperta di un'esperienza misticheggiante procede senza che nulla venga lasciato al caso; i particolari forniti dall'autore nel suo ennesimo viaggio, costituisco, infatti, itinerari realistici lungo i quali l'autore/autrice si identifica, ritrovando luoghi e immagini reali a lui/lei cari: sono le coste del remoto arcipelago scozzese di St Kilda e Ushant, isola del canale britannico a nord della Francia; sono Achill, la più grande isola ad ovest dell'Irlanda e la gallese St. Bride's Bay nel Pembrokeshire. Fu, in questo caso, la più pura vena celtica di Macleod a riemergere da uno spazio riservato al mito e al folklore, all'aspetto visionario delle sue creazioni e al contemporaneo e vivido riaffiorare di ricordi e osservazioni personali, protagonisti tutti di una storia spirituale narrata da un moderno *wandering Breton Minstrel* che Macleod stessa definì "as the soul of the Celt who wanders homeless to-day."

È all'interno della raccolta (composta da un prologo e dalle sezioni *By Sundown Shores, The Lynne of Dreams, The Wind, Silence and Love, Barabal, Sheumas, The Sea-Madness*, e *Earth Fire and Water*) che si palesa una probabile risoluzione della sua perpetua ricerca di "un ritorno a casa." Proprio nella sezione che diede il titolo alla raccolta leggiamo: "But there are poets who have no name and no country, because they are named by the secret name of the longing of many minds, and mysteriously come from and pass to the Land of Heart's Desire, which is their own land."

O ancora, dalla sezione *The Wind, Silence and Love*:

> With most of us the shaping influences are the common sweet influences of motherhood and fatherhood, the airs of home, the place and manner of childhood. But these are not for all, and may be adverse, and in some degree absent. Even when a child is fortunate in love and home, it may be spiritually alien from these: it may dimly discern love rather as a mystery dwelling in sunlight and moonlight, or in the light that lies on quiet meadows, woods, quiet shores: may find a more intimate sound of home in the wind whispering in the grass, or when a sighing travels through the wilderness of leaves, or when an unseen wave moans in the pine.

Si trattò dunque di elaborare una nuova geografia, una *literary geography* del tutto rivoluzionaria, che sfociò nella creazione di un'omonima raccolta nel 1904, all'interno della quale natura e cultura, spirito e corpo costituirono percorsi nuovi, ridisegnando il mondo terrestre facendo della letteratura e dell'arte lo strumento prediletto di una nuova geografia dello spirito (lo testimoniano i titoli altamente significativi delle sezioni della raccolta: *The Country of George Meredith, The Country of Stevenson, Dickens-land, Scott-land, The Country of George Eliot, Thackeray-land, The Bronte Country, Aylwin-land, The Carlyle Country, The Literary Geography of the English Lakes, The Literary Geography of the Thames, The Literary Geography of the Lake of Geneva*).

A tal proposito poi: "According to the critic in *The World*: 'It was a characteristically original idea of the author to combine descriptions of certain localities with criticisms and appreciations of those famous writers who had identified themselves therewith. It gives one a fresher and keener insight.'" (*A Memoir* II: 273-274)

Solo qualche anno prima della sua scomparsa, dunque, Sharp approdò ad una nuova prospettiva descrittiva, all'interno della quale i luoghi e gli spazi non possono che proporre in maniera perpetua un'intima identificazione con l'animo che li attraversa, li impersona, li respira.

## Works Cited

Alaya, Flavia. *William Sharp – "Fiona Macleod" 1855-1905*. Cambridge, Massachusetts: Harvard University Press, 1970.

Macleod, Fiona. *By Sundown Shores* (1900). Portland Maine: George Loring Press, Thomas B. Mosher, c.1902; i riferimenti alla preziosa raccolta contenuti all'interno di questo contributo sono stati tratti dal testo integralmente disponibile al seguente URL: http://www.sundown.pair.com/

\_\_\_\_\_. *Poems and Dramas*. New York: Duffield, 1914.

\_\_\_\_\_. *The Divine Adventure*. London: Chapman & Hall, 1900.

Sharp, Elizabeth. A. *William Sharp, Fiona Macleod: A Memoir*. London: William Heinemann, 1910; i riferimenti all'interno di questo contributo sono tratti dall'edizione, Sharp, Elizabeth A., *William Sharp, Fiona Macleod: A Memoir*, Voll I-II, La Vergne: Kessinger Publishing, 2002.

Sharp, William. *Literary Geography*. London: Pall Mall, 1904.

# La Traversata: Italian Immigrant Accounts of Ocean Crossings[1]

## Michele Campanini

MUCH HAS BEEN WRITTEN ON the topic of Italian emigration to America in the nineteenth and twentieth centuries. But despite the vast amount of research on the topic, the ocean crossing itself, perhaps the biggest single event in the immigrant experience, is also one of the least studied. Though it permanently marked their lives, once they arrived in the New World, immigrants, for their part, seemed to have left the memories of the journey on board the ship.

During my many trips to Canada, I met many Italian immigrants who left Italy in the 1950s and 1960s. They were all happy to tell me about their present lives, the beautiful houses they had bought, and the brilliant careers of their children. But nobody seemed to want to discuss the ocean crossing – the days they spent inside that "immense steel vessel," as author Pascal D'Angelo called it.

It was for this reason that I always pictured the crossing experience to be an ordeal – one that every immigrant wanted to remove from his or her mind. It appears, however, that I was wrong, and for this I have to thank Antonio, a Sicilian immigrant. Antonio let me understand that the picture I had formed – nourished by the books I had read on the topic and my own bias – was misleading. I met Antonio on a flight from Rome to Toronto; he was sitting next to me. He seemed quite old, perhaps in his eighties, but still strong. Dark eyes, olive skin, big hands. He was born in Sicily and immigrated to Canada in the 1950s when he was a young man.

Antonio didn't seem comfortable on the plane, nor was I. I had some trouble, as the plane ran into an air pocket. He saw that I was nervous, looked at me and smiled. He spoke to me in Italian: "Lucky you, travelling by plane! The first time I came to Canada, I had to board an old rusty ship in Naples. These air pockets are nothing compared to the rough water! We went through building-size waves!" Prompted by the air turbulence, Antonio began to tell me the story of his ocean crossing.

Through his recollections, I began to understand what that voyage represented for him and the hundreds of other Italians with whom he was travelling. I understood that in those days, sailing through the middle of nowhere, made him feel like he was almost hanging in time, balanced between a hastily abandoned past and a suddenly precarious future. He didn't know anything about Canada, except for what he had heard in his tiny village, lost in Sicily's inland mountains: "In Canadà ci stavano tante belle gherle e i money" (In Canada, there were many beautiful girls and money). Warily, for he had been widowed many years, he told me about love affairs that had taken place on the journey across the waters. Contrary to my expectations, he seemed to remember every detail from that cruise – dates, sounds, scents.

After that particular journey to Canada with Antonio, I realized that it was worth trying to investigate other stories like his – to reconstruct the crossings, the daily life on board, and the immigrants' memories and feelings – the kinds of stories which had never really been heard.

I set out to interview elderly Italian-Canadians, mostly around the Greater Toronto Area, about their crossings into the country. It usually took some time to gain the individuals' trust and get them to remember. But as they began to feel comfortable, they inevitably began to recount their memories. The stories were unexpected and at times astonishing.

At the same time I started looking for more stories through other primary sources such as diaries, letters, and autobiographies. I did so both in Italy, thanks to institutions like the Paolo Cresci Foundation in Lucca, and in Canada, through institutions like Canada's Immigration Museum at Pier 21 in Halifax.

I also searched through literature that was based on real events and memories. I discovered how helpful cinema could be for my research by watching movies like *Nuovomondo* by Emanuele Crialese and *La leggenda del pianista sull'oceano* by Giuseppe Tornatore. I also viewed *The Immigrant* by Charlie Chaplin and *Titanic* by James Cameron. These diverse research materials were the key that allowed me to enter the immigrant's world.

Through first-person accounts, I was introduced to immigrants from the late nineteenth century. Francesco Sartori of Veneto, for example, wrote a letter in 1877 to his relatives, reporting that he and the ship's other passengers lived compressed as in a beehive (as quoted by Emilio Franzina). Rosa Cavallieri, from Lombardia, who crossed the ocean in 1884, wrote in her autobiography about the pitiful accommodations: "All us poor people had to go down through a hole to the bottom of the ship. And in that time the third class on the boat was not like now. The girls and women and men had to sleep all together in the same room. The men and girls even had to sleep in the same bed with only those little half-boards in between to keep us from rolling together. But I was lucky. I had two girls sleeping next to me."

Through Cavallieri I learned about terrible storms when "the sky grew black and the ocean came over the deck." I could imagine the hundreds of passengers trapped in the dark steerage like rats in a hole, without air and light. I spoke to many immigrants who recounted getting sick because of the storms and fearing that the ship would sink, and praying to God.

But when the sea was calm, the crossing could be an enjoyable experience. In fact, once the passengers had done the few daily chores required by life on board a ship, there was a lot of free time. The immigrants used to spend those leisurely hours playing cards, throwing dice, or just looking at the ocean from the upper deck, gazing down at the fish. One of the most common pastimes was to play music and dance. Rosa Cavallieri remembers:

> One man had a *concertina*, and the ones who knew how to dance were dancing to entertain the others. Me, I was the best one. There was no one there to scold me and tell me what to do, so I danced with all my *paesani* who knew how. I even danced with some of the Polish and the French. We were like floating in a cloud in the middle of nowhere, and when I was dancing I forgot for a little while that I was the wife of Santino going to him in America.

The most common activity for men, both bachelors and married, seemed to be looking at women. When there was some good-looking girl on board, many tried to get her attention. In the words of Rosa Cavallieri: "We were in the middle of nowhere," far away from relatives, mothers-in-law and husbands-by-proxy. That was the point. Being away from the mainland made people feel free even if, in fact, they were not.

When it came to onboard love affairs, what happened during the crossings mostly remained locked in the immigrants' memories for years, maybe even for a lifetime. There was an unspoken agreement: once on land, everyone went his or her own way without looking back – New World, new beginning.

Osvaldo Zappa, who emigrated to Canada in 1956, writes in his autobiography, *Giovanni's Journey*, about the attraction he felt towards Anna, an Italian woman crossing the ocean to join her fiancé:

> I liked Anna more and more; I think she felt the same about me. We sought each other's company. When I thought about her going to get married to some other fellow in Ontario, it started to bother me somewhat. She seemed to be sincerely attracted to me. Very often we remained very late at the bar, sipping drinks and chatting. Occasionally, we would step outside on the wintry deck holding hands.

As the port of Halifax drew near, Zappa knew that his time with Anna was running out. He writes: "Anna would be on the train with me at least as far as Sudbury, the end of her journey. 'She will vanish as if she had never existed,' I thought."

An Italian immigrant from Molise who wanted to remain anonymous told me a story about a girl from his village who, in the 1950s, arrived in Canada engaged to an Italian-Canadian man. She supposedly had left Italy a virgin. She arrived in Halifax, her fiancé and family there to welcome her. On her wedding night, however, her husband discovered that she was not a virgin! She was roughed up and sent back to Italy on the first available ship, dishonoured for the rest of her life. It seems something had happened during the crossing...

Conditions on ships between the end of the nineteenth century and fifty years later improved a lot for the third-class passengers. In his diary, Tommaso Bordonaro describes life on the ship in 1947. He was especially enthusiastic about the food that was served onboard, in terms of both quality and quantity. There was pasta, various kinds of meat, coffee, butter (which in Italy, he says, was extremely rare), sugar, honey, and fruit. In the Italy of the times, this variety of food could only be had by the rich: "Il caffè ed il latte si usava come si usava l'acqua in Italia quando si era in campagna. E questa vita per tutto il viaggio." (We drank coffee and milk the way people drink water in the Italian countryside. This was true for the entire journey.) Bordonaro reports that many passengers had brought their own food for the crossing: cheese, biscuits, almonds, liquor, lemons, and oranges. When they finally got around to opening the bags, the food had rotted.

Many unpleasant aspects of life onboard, such as fear of the ocean and storms at sea, were common among travellers in both centuries, as was the recurring theme of the sorrow for what was being left behind and the uncertainties for the future. But the enjoyable side of the journey, however short lived, cannot be understated.

Indeed, by the 1960s the price of intercontinental flights became affordable, and the unique world of the immigrant ships began to disappear. Hundreds of ships fell into disuse or were turned into cruise liners. By the 1970s, Italian immigration had ebbed considerably. Emigration as a mass event all but ceased, or was turned into a solitary process. In a flight that lasts a few hours, there is no time to socialize with other immigrants, to make friends, to share feelings, fears, and regrets.

The ocean crossing was not just an ordeal, as is commonly thought, but also represented for many immigrants the opportunity for freedom: sailing on the calm sea, allowed them to sing, dance, share dreams and desires, make new friends, start over, and sometimes, even find new loves.

## Note

1. First published in English in *Accenti Magazine*, Issue 20, Fall 2010, 18-20.

# Contributors

**Annalisa Bonomo** vive a Nicosia, in provincia di Enna. È Dottore di Ricerca in Studi Inglesi ed Angloamericani e Ricercatrice di Lingua Inglese e Traduzione presso l'Università di Enna "Kore." Autrice dei volumi *Philip Pullman: "Finzione originale" e "verità tradotta" in His Dark Materials* (2009), e *Discutere di plurilinguismo nell'epoca della complessità* (2012), ha pubblicato numerosi articoli in ambito linguistico e letterario.

**John Calabro** is an educator, a publisher, a writer, and president of Quattro Books Inc., an independent Toronto press. He is also the president of The Association for Art and Social Change. Calabro's *Bellecour*, Guernica Editions (2005), was named by *The Globe and Mail*'s First Fiction Reviewer as one of the top 5 First Fiction of the year. His short stories, essays and reviews have appeared in many literary magazines and journals. He published *the Cousin* in 2009.

**Michele Campanini** has an MA and PhD from the University of Siena. He teaches Italian Literature in high school as well as Italian language for foreign PhD students at the University of Siena. He is the author of *Emigration Accounts and Renderings of Ocean Crossings: Memories, Stories, Voices*, published in Italian in 2010. In 2012, he was postdoctoral fellow at the University of Siena as a research team member of the European project "Playing identities" about "migration, creolization, creation."

**Licia Canton** holds a Ph.D. from Université de Montréal. She is the author of *Almond Wine and Fertility*, a collection of short stories for women and their men. She is also a literary translator and critic, and editor-in-chief of *Accenti Magazine* – www.accenti.ca. She is (co)editor of seven volumes on multiethnic writing, including two books on the internment of Italian Canadians – *Behind Barbed Wire* (creative works) and *Beyond Barbed Wire* (essays), available at www.guernicaeditions.com/free_ebooks.php.

## CONTRIBUTORS

**Maria Giuseppina (Giusy) Cesari** is a legal translator at the Ministry of Justice and at the Prosecutor General Office at the Supreme Court in Rome. She has worked as a teacher at universities and training institutions. She has a PhD (with a thesis on Italian Canadian and Italian American Literature) from the University of Macerata. She published articles for *la Vallée* and for the Marche Region. She lives in San Benedetto del Tronto.

**Pietro Corsi,** born in Molise in 1937, was a translator and co-creator of radio programs for RAI, and worked for *Il Cittadino Canadese*. He was the Executive Vice President of Princess Cruises until 1992. He published *La Giobba* (Enne, 1982) and *Winter in Montreal* (Guernica, 2000), winner of the 2002 Bressani Prize. His most recent book is *Halifax: The Other Door to America* (Guernica, 2102), and soon to be published: *Neruda, il corvo bianco, il gatto nero*.

**Giovanni Costa** (1940-2011) was born in Vizzini, Sicily. A member of the AICW since 1989, he read his poetry at the conference in Atri in June 2010. He passed away shortly thereafter, on February 3, 2011. For three decades he taught at Laval University's École de Langues in Quebec City. He published four collections of poetry: *Impressioni in terre amiche* (1989), *Parlami di stelle, Fammi sognare/Speak to me of Stars, Let Me dream* (1994), *Alternanze, Alternances, Alternations* (1999) and *Al di là dell'orizzonte, Au delà de l'horizon, Beyond the Horizon* (2004). His poetry also appears in several anthologies.

**Domenic Cusmano** is a Montreal publisher, writer and communications consultant. He is the co-founder and publisher of *Accenti Magazine*, an English-language national quarterly whose mission is to give expression to Canada's Italian heritage. He is also the publisher of Longbridge Books, a publishing house launched in 2007 whose mandate is to promote fiction and non-fiction that convey Canada's multicultural character.

**Marisa De Franceschi** is the author of *Surface Tension* (Guernica, 1994), the short story collection *Family Matters* (Guernica, 2001) and editor of the anthology *Pillars of Lace* (Guernica, 1998). Her short stories, articles and book reviews have appeared in a variety of publications, including *Canadian Author & Bookman, Pure Fiction* and *Accenti Magazine*. Her most recent book is *Random Thoughts: Poetry and Prose Sketches* (Longbridge Books, 2010).

**Mike Dell'Aquila** received a BA in English from Penn State University and an MA in English from Brooklyn College. His writing has appeared in a variety of print and online publications including *Paterson Literary Review*, *VIA: Voices in Italian Americana*, *Florida English Literary Journal*, *Italian Americana*, and *Kalliope: A Penn State Literary Journal*. Mike also maintains a blog at http://mikedellaquila.blogspot.com.

**Alberto Mario DeLogu** è nato in Sardegna e risiede a Montreal. Agronomo ed economista, autore di saggi ed articoli scientifici, è stato caporedattore di *Trentagiorni* e collabora con Italia a tavola, About Food e l'Altra Voce. Ha pubblicato a Toronto *La biodiversità delle parole* (2003) e *Cetre appese* (2004), e *Sardignolo* (2011). Vincitore del premio Gramsci 2005 con S'iskeras e del premio Città di Salò 2006 con Transamanti.

**Delia De Santis** is the author of the collection *Fast Forward and Other Stories* (Longbridge Books, 2008). She has co-edited anthologies and published many short stories in literary magazines. She is a member of the Association of Italian Canadian Writers, the Canadian Authors Association, and the Writers' Union of Canada.

**Gil Fagiani**'s published collections of poetry include *Serfs of Psychiatry* (Finishing Line Press, 2012), *Chianti in Connecticut* (Bordighera Press, 2010), and *A Blanquito in El Barrio* (Rain Mountain Press, 2009). He has translated into English poetry written in Italian and Abruzzese dialect. Gil co-curates the Italian American Writers' Association's readings at the Cornelia Street Café and is a founding member of the Vito Marcantonio Forum.

**Nino Famà** was born in Italy and came to Canada at the age of eighteen. He has published many books and numerous articles including two works of fiction. *La stanza segreta* (2004) was published in Italian, then translated into English by Leonard Sbrocchi and Douglas Campbell and published by LEGAS (2008). A collection of short stories, *Don Gaudenzio e altre Storie*, was published in Italy in 1996.

**Venera Fazio** was born in Bafia, Sicily, and now lives in Bright's Grove, Ontario. She has co-edited six anthologies relating to Italian/Italian immigrant culture, including *Sweet Lemons 2: International Writings with a Sicilian Accent* (Legas, 2010). Her poetry and prose have been published in literary magazines in Canada, Italy and the United States. She has co-edited a recent issue of *Descant*, dedicated to the island of Sicily.

**Frank Giorno** lives in Timmins, Ontario, and writes about mining and First Nations. His essay "Internee 328," co-written with James McCreath, appears in *Beyond Barbed Wire* (Guernica, 2012). His poem "Horses for Mussolini" appears in *Behind Barbed Wire* (Guernica, 2012). Two books of poetry, *Elvis in America* (2006) and *Arrivederci! Plastic Covered Couch* (2008) were published by Lyricalmyrical Press. He is the founder of the Timmins Voices Reading Series and *Northern Voices Journal*.

**Gabriella Iacobucci** ha tradotto in italiano autori canadesi tra cui Nino Ricci e Mary di Michele. La sua associazione, Molise d'Autore, si prefigge di divulgare attraverso una serie di iniziative le opere degli scrittori stranieri di origine molisana. L'ultima, Biblioteche Aperte (patrocinata dalla Regione Molise e dall'Ambasciata del Canada), sta portando nei piccoli centri del Molise la letteratura italocanadese.

**Elena Lamberti** teaches American and Canadian Literature at the University of Bologna, Italy. She co-edited several volumes including *Memories and Representations of War in Europe: The Case of WW1 and WW2* (Rodopi, 2009). Her volumes include the award winning *Marshall McLuhan: Tra letteratura, arti e media* (Bruno Mondadori, 2000); *"the transatlantic review": Note sulla rivista che traghettò gli Yankees in Europa*, (Asterisco, 2012); *Marshall McLuhan's Mosaic: Probing the Literary Origins of Media Studies* (U. of Toronto Press, 2012).

**Maria Lisella**'s Pushcart-Prize-nominated work appears in her two chapbooks, *Two Naked Feet* (Poets Wear Prada), and *Amore on Hope Street* (Finishing Line Press). Her work has been published in *The New York Quarterly*, translated into French in *Liqueur 44* and anthologized. She is a member of the online poetry circle Brevitas and co-curates the Italian American Writers Association's readings at Cornelia St. Café. Her collection *Thieves in the Family* (New York Quarterly Books) is forthcoming.

**Ernesto Livorni** is a professor at the University of Wisconsin – Madison. He has published *Avanguardia e tradizione: Ezra Pound e Giuseppe Ungaretti* (Florence: Casa Editrice Le Lettere, 1998) and the translation of Ted Hughes' *Cave-Birds: Un dramma alchemico della caverna* (Milan: Arnoldo Mondadori Editore, 2001). Author of three collections of poetry, he is the founding editor of *L'ANELLO che non tiene: Journal of Modern Italian Literature*.

**Darlene Madott** is a Toronto lawyer and writer. She is the author of *Bottled Roses* (1985), *Mazilli's Shoes* (1997) and *Joy, Joy, Why Do I Sing?* (2004). Winner of the 2002 Paolucci Prize of the Italian American Writers' Association, Darlene Madott has also won the 2008 Bressani

Literary Award for the title story of *Making Olives and Other Family Secrets* (Longbridge Books, 2008). Her most recent publication is *Stations of the Heart* (Exile Editions, 2012), which includes the story "Waiting," shortlisted for the Gloria Vanderbilt/Exile Editions literary award.

**Michael Mirolla**'s publications include two novels – the Bressani prize-winning *Berlin* and *The Facility*; the novella *The Ballad of Martin B.*; two short story collections *The Formal Logic of Emotion* (translated into Italian), and *The Giulio Metaphysics III*; and several collections of poetry. Scheduled for publication in 2013: the poetry collection *The House on 14th Avenue*. Along with partner Connie McParland, Michael runs Guernica Editions, a Canadian publishing house.

**Caroline Morgan Di Giovanni** came to the University of Toronto from Philadelphia, in 1966. By marriage to Alberto Di Giovanni, she became part of the Italian Canadian community in Toronto. She is the author of *Looking at Renaissance Paintings and Other Poems* (2008). She is the editor of *Bravo!* (2012), a collection of prose and poetry, and two editions of the anthology *Italian Canadian Voices* (1984 and 2006).

**Linda Morra** is the Chair of the Department of English at Bishop's University. Her publications include *Corresponding Influence: Selected Letters of Emily Carr and Ira Dilworth* (UTP 2006) and a co-edited collection of essays, *Basements and Attics, Closets and Cyberspace: Explorations in Canadian Women's Archives* (WLUP 2012).

**Oriana Palusci**, full professor of English at the University of Naples, "L'Orientale," has published on nineteenth and twentieth century women writers, utopian literature, cultural studies, postcolonial studies, translation studies and tourism. She has edited the Italian translation of Canadian writers (Atwood, Laurence, Engel, Munro, Merril) and is the author of essays on Italian-Canadian language and culture. She has recently edited *Translating Virginia Woolf* (2012).

**Gianna Patriarca** was born in Ceprano (Frosinone) and immigrated to Canada in 1960. Her poetry has been published in anthologies, journals and magazines; broadcast on radio and television; and adapted for the stage. She was runner-up to the Milton Acorn People's Poetry Award in 1995. She has published nine collections of poetry, including *My Etruscan Face* (2007) and *Too Much Love* (2012). The collection of short stories, *All My Fallen Angelas*, is forthcoming.

**Maria Cristina Seccia** is a PhD student in Translation Studies at Bangor University, Wales. Her PhD project consists of the translation into Italian of *The Lion's Mouth* (1984) by Caterina Edwards and a theoretical commentary. It aims to show how it is important for the translator to preserve the hybridity of such a source text in which the author's Italian origins are deeply reflected both from a cultural and linguistic point of view.

**Maria Tognan** obtained a PhD from the University of Udine. Her research in Comparative Literature focused on cultural encounters and identity inscriptions in the fictional and creative non-fictional works of Caterina Edwards and Janice Kulyk-Keefer. Tognan currently teaches EFL in Italian secondary schools. She has published academic essays as well as interactive materials for the teaching of literature in the EFL classroom.

**Osvaldo G. Zappa** was born in Italy and educated at the Istituto Tecnico for Geometri in Sulmona, Aquila. He immigrated to Canada in 1956. He worked at different jobs until 1962 when he enrolled in the Engineering Faculty at UBC. He left school to work in the forest industry until his retirement in the year 2000. In 2010 he published a memoir titled *Giovanni's Journey*.

**Jim Zucchero** teaches Canadian Studies and works as an academic counsellor at King's University College at Western University. He earned a PhD in English at Western and has published creative non-fiction and numerous essays on Italian-Canadian writers. He co-edited *Reflections on Culture* (2010) and two books published in 2012: *Beyond Barbed Wire: Essays on the Internment of Italian Canadians* and *Behind Barbed Wire: Creative Works on the Internment of Italian Canadians*, available at www.guernicaeditions.com/free_ebooks.php.